"It's always been _____ _____ _____ _____
daunting than ever in this time of c_ _____ _____
insights into how to balance the polarity between caring for
yourself and _____ _____ _____ wn
deep experie _____ _____ s of
encouragem _____

_____ _ PARISH

"With cando _____ red
lessons learr _____ e than
25 years. See _____ y, he
offers sugge _____ es
clergy and l _____ ng
healthy relat _____ nd
recommend _____ ders
who can ma _____

_____ RECTOR,
INISTERS

"A compellir _____
organization _____ ority
to soul-care, _____
many years _____ of
talking to pe _____ ns
and answers _____ out to
Give Up. Rea _____ matter
the step of th _____

_____ NDENT,
_____ HURCH

"Travis Colli___ ___ ___ ___ ___ ___ to the illness of
lethargy that seems to plague modern ministry. Mixing
powerful quotes, excellent biblical application, and a wonderful
array of real-life stories from a career in ministry, he speaks the
language ministers can hear. Travis has lived the day-to-day life
of a minister with grace and skill, and he brings that wisdom
to these pages. Reading these pages is like reading a working
pastor's diary, and you will be blessed by the insights he has
gleaned along the way."

—WILLIAM G. WILSON, PRESIDENT,
THE CENTER FOR HEALTHY CHURCHES

"Travis Collins' latest book blends practicality with reality. It is a must-read for ministers and lay leadership to understand the complexities of one of the most demanding occupations."

— MAURICE GRAHAM, FOUNDER AND EXECUTIVE DIRECTOR, SHEPHERD'S STAFF MINISTRY

"With keen encouragement and practical insights, Travis Collins offers the young (and experienced) parish minister an honest and challenging 'inside look' into what it means to follow God's call and minister in the local church. This experienced pastor offers candid, at times confessional, descriptions of what a minister will or does encounter in ministry, adding to it a solid measure of the privilege, trust, and responsibility involved in the sacred work of shepherding. The section on pastoral leadership is by itself worth the reader's time."

—DAN BAGBY, BAPTIST THEOLOGICAL SEMINARY AT RICHMOND

"Ministry is hard. It always has been, and always will be. But most things that are worthwhile are hard. Travis Collins knows this because he's been there and back again. Along the way Travis learned how to thrive in ministry, and he wants to share his story with those who are just starting out, or just about to pack it in. If only I had such a mentor when I was just starting out, my own path might have been much smoother. Read this book, meditate on its stories and practical advice. It might just save your life in ministry."

—STAN GRAHAM, FOUNDING PASTOR, PATHWAYS CHURCH, FOREST HILL, MARYLAND

"Travis Collins has written a book that is ideal for both new and seasoned ministers. I find that I fall in both categories, having served in ministry positions for 35 years, and now having begun my first pastorate. The phrase 'keep watch,' from Acts 20, is a recurring theme in the book and one that I will return to time and time again. As I face new experiences as a pastor, that phrase will remain in the forefront of my ministry. Thank you, Travis, for the challenging reminder."

—Jane Hull, Pastor,
Union Christian Church (Disciples of Christ),
Watkinsville, Georgia

"Travis Collins has provided pastors a gift through his honest, transparent, and authentic disclosure of the incredible joy and despair of serving congregations. He takes us on a journey through the heartbeat of a pastor. A must-read for clergy whose energy for ministry needs a booster."

—Steven N. Scoggin, President of CareNet, Inc.

"Collins presents the sharp and pressing realities of the challenge of ministering in today's church and world. His seasoned perspective allows him to write with transparency, realism, and extreme passion and hope for ministers. I commend the book to you as a companion for the spiritual journey of leadership, mentoring, discipleship, and self-care. A careful reading offers deep assurance that God is with us in the tough days and the times of celebration as leadership and ministry unfolds in distinctive ways in a variety of ministry contexts."

—Edward H. Hammett,
Author of Recovering Hope for Your Church

FOR
MINISTERS
about to START

...or about to
GIVE UP

Travis Collins

Scripture quotations marked (NIV) are taken from the HOLY BIBLE, NEW INTERNATIONAL VERSION®. NIV®. Copyright © 1973, 1978, 1984 by International Bible Society. Used by permission of Zondervan Publishing House. All rights reserved.

Bible quotations marked NRSV are from the *New Revised Standard Version Bible*, copyright 1989, Division of Christian Education of the National

Council of the Churches of Christ in the United States of America. Used by permission. All rights reserved.

Scripture marked NASB is taken from the *NEW AMERICAN STANDARD BIBLE* ®, © Copyright The Lockman Foundation 1960, 1962, 1963, 1968, 1971, 1972, 1973, 1975, 1977, 1995. Used by permission.

Biblical quotations marked REB are from *The Revised English Bible copyright* © Oxford University Press and Cambridge University Press 1989. *The Revised English Bible with the Apocrypha* first published 1989.

Quotations marked Message are from *The Message* by Eugene H. Peterson, copyright © 1993, 1994, 1995, 1996, 2000, 2001, 2002. Used by permission of NavPress Publishing Group. All rights reserved.

Cover art: ShutterStock
Cover design: Scribe, Inc.

www.TheColumbiaPartnership.org
www.TCPBooks.com

Print: 978-08272-32280 EPUB: 978-08272-32297 EPDF: 978-08272-32303

Library of Congress Cataloging-in-Publication Data
Collins, Travis.
For ministers about to start... or about to give up / by Travis Collins.
   pages cm
Includes bibliographical references and index.
ISBN 978-0-8272-1095-0 (pbk. : alk. paper)
1. Pastoral theology. I. Title.

BV4011.3.C65 2014
253--dc23
                         2014030292

To the vocational ministers alongside whom I've served.

Contents

Editor's Foreword

**Inspiration and Wisdom for
21st-Century Christian Leaders**

You have chosen wisely in deciding to read and learn from a book published by TCP Books from The Columbia Partnership.

We publish for

- Congregational leaders who desire to serve with greater faithfulness, effectiveness, and innovation.
- Christian ministers who seek to pursue and sustain excellence in ministry service.
- Members of congregations who desire to reach their full kingdom potential.
- Christian leaders who desire to use a coach approach in their ministry.
- Denominational and parachurch leaders who want to come alongside affiliated congregations in a servant leadership role.
- Consultants and coaches who desire to increase their learning concerning the congregations and Christian leaders they serve.

TCP Books is a sharing knowledge strategy of The Columbia Partnership, a community of Christian leaders seeking to transform the capacity of the North American Church to pursue and sustain vital Christ-centered ministry.

Primarily serving congregations, denominations, educational institutions, leadership development programs, and parachurch organizations, TCP also seeks to connect with individuals, businesses, and other organizations seeking a Christ-centered spiritual focus.

We welcome your comments on these books, and we welcome your suggestions for new subject areas and authors we ought to consider.

**George Bullard, Senior Editor, TCP Books
The Columbia Partnership**
332 Valley Springs Road, Columbia, SC 292236934
Voice: 803.622.0923, Website: www.TheColumbiaPartnership.org

The Leadership Dance

I remember a day years ago when someone I trust completely, and who is old enough to be my mom, asked me (I mean really asked me) how I was doing. Suddenly, I couldn't speak. I felt a huge toad well up in my gullet. Then I heard myself mumble, "I don't think I can do this anymore."

I was the pastor of the best church I knew, yet I was struggling under the threat of burnout and disillusionment. My ministry passion was leaking. My shepherd's heart was deflating.

I made it back from that brink and went on to have a rewarding and effective ministry there. Yet the memory of that day (and a few others like it)—when I wondered if I might step away from the pastorate to escape its pressures—is still vivid.

Spiritual leadership never has been easy. Throughout history, neither spiritual leaders nor the spiritually led have always been happy about the way the arrangement works.

The Church is what we might call a "volunteer organization." It doesn't function effectively without unpaid people doing the bulk of the work. And when the volunteers (members) are doing the bulk of the work, it seems the volunteers should make the bulk of the decisions, right? It's called "buy-in."

Except, the leaders (i.e., vocational ministers) carry the bulk of the responsibility for the effectiveness of the church and ultimately will answer for how they lead it (Heb. 13:17). So it stands to reason that the ministers should make the bulk of the decisions, right? It's called good management.

See the problem? And that's just one of the complicated issues in this dance between clergy and laity. Sometimes the differences between the pulpit and the pew are theological or political. Sometimes certain congregations have developed a pattern of being hard on their ministers. Sometimes certain ministers have developed a pattern of being hard on their congregations. Sometimes everyone is on edge because of external political or economic tensions. Legion are the sources of congregational struggles. From Moses and the Israelites to Paul and the Corinthian

Christians to all who have served the church since then, this thing called spiritual leadership has been thorny.

So I'm not surprised that the odds are against you making it to your retirement as a vocational minister. The statistics aren't encouraging, as I'll show you later. Yet, I'd love to help you beat the odds, serve with real joy, and be a truly biblical minister. I'd be delighted if God would use me to help you serve joyfully and effectively well into your autumn years.

I'm not so presumptuous that I think I can tell you how to do what God has called you to do in your particular setting. For one thing, my batting average is not 1,000. When it comes to difficult church situations, I've been up to bat a bunch, and I've struck out more than I care to remember. For another thing, our contexts, our gifts, and our weaknesses are different. What works for me might not work for you. Still, we both know there is value when human beings on common paths share their experiences and discoveries with one another. It's a bit like being the second golfer to putt the hole. Things like dips, slopes, and speed of the green are easier to judge if you've looked over the shoulder of one who putted before you, even if the other golfer missed the putt. My three-plus decades of Christian vocational ministry and what I've learned during that time may help you play through the holes better.

I am assuming that many of you are either thinking of beginning or thinking of quitting vocational ministry. Perhaps you're either fairly fired up about vocational ministry or fairly fed up with it. If God would bless me with the opportunity to somehow help you be the minister God created you to be, to help you find and follow what the Bible says about how we are to live out our calling, and to keep you in the game, then I'd be more than honored.

Before I go any further, I want you to know that I love the Church. I'm committed to the Church and want to pour myself into the Church's health, mission, and future. The Church is my people, and in the depth of my being I believe the Church is the best hope for the world. I gladly take my place in the imperfect, idiosyncratic, international family called the Church. At the same time, I also know that serving her is not for the faint of heart.

A text that has been of great benefit to me is Acts 20:28— words from the apostle Paul to fellow ministers in the trenches. Paul's counsel is not limited by time or geography. Its clarity and practicality can benefit those of us who lead and serve churches today, if we will but listen. I am so convinced of this text's importance that I have chosen to outline this book according to the flow of that Pauline piece of guidance.

This book springs from the core of my soul. For me this book is not an academic exercise or a little thing to do on the side. I believe it is one of the most important things I have ever done. Contributing to the health and effectiveness of my fellow ministers and their churches might turn out to be my greatest Kingdom service.

You honor me by reading this work. I honestly pray God will use this to make you both a better minister and more glad that you are a minister.

Travis Collins

1

What You Do Is Hard

"I've worked in state government, a Fortune 500 company, and even a political campaign. The worst experience I've ever had at a job was working full-time in ministry."

—JOHN, A FORMER EXECUTIVE PASTOR[1]

Now that we're rolling, let me state the obvious but necessary: What you do is hard—*really* hard.

In the February 25, 2014, issue of *Forbes* online (at Forbes.com), Rob Asghar ranked the "10 Hardest Leadership Roles." Coming in at number five was "Pastor, Rabbi, Mullah or Other Holy Leader."[2] What you do is hard. It is an honor. It can certainly be thrilling at times. And we often see the gift of God's mercy in the work. But it is still hard. When I talk about this with ministers, I hear shocking stories of abuse: from slashed tires to physical threats made to children and spouses. The job has struggles and hurts that many jobs do not. It can be so tough that theologian Stanley Hauerwas has declared, "God is a nasty employer."[3] Of course it's true that lots of other vocations are hard as well, so I don't want to over-dramatize what ministers face. This is not a whine fest. Nevertheless, the fact that many vocations are difficult does not negate the often painful truth: What you do is hard.

Let's face it: (1) there is nothing quite as ugly as Christians acting badly; (2) no hurt hurts quite like church hurt; and (3) when you combine unhealthy, unhappy people with the accommodating ("we have to be nice even to the mean folks") environment of church, things can go sideways quickly. This is why a lot of the folks who start out optimistically in ministry will spend most of their vocational lives selling shoes, real estate, or retirement plans. Many will be terminated by their congregations because they either didn't "produce" or they couldn't do important things like maintain sexual purity. Many ministers will grow so tired of the congregational bickering over trivial things that they will walk away shaking their heads incredulously. Many will leave their ministry posts with nowhere to go because to remain would jeopardize the well-being of their families. J. R. Woodward reported that "Bobby Clinton and his team, after studying over a thousand biblical, historical and contemporary leaders' lives, discovered that 70 percent of those who begin their spiritual journey well end poorly."[4]

Lots of newly called ministers decide at the outset to serve in some ministry role other than on the staff of an existing church. They've heard too many bad stories from those who've been there.

What you do is hard.

New studies seem to come out monthly noting the crisis of hurt and burnout among vocational ministers. Some data are communicating things such as: "The majority of American ministers are suffering from burnout"; "Fifty percent of pastors surveyed are so discouraged that they would leave the ministry if they could, but have no other way of making a living"; and, "Eighty percent of seminary and Bible school graduates who enter the ministry will leave the ministry within the first five years."[5]

People are describing the current situation with words like *epic proportions, scourge,* and *plague.* We clearly have a big problem. Bill Wilson, President of the Center for Healthy Churches, called it a "pandemic." I'm talking about a plague of pastors hurting so deeply that they are leaving vocational ministry, thinking about leaving, or choosing to remain in vocational ministry with such an albatross of discouragement around their necks that they are not reaching their leadership potential.

I found this "pastor burnout joke" on the website www. pastorburnout.com:

> Jesus made a quick return to earth for a visit. He came upon a lame man, had compassion on him, and healed his leg.

Further down the road, our Lord came upon a blind man, had compassion on him, and healed him.

A little further down the road, Jesus came upon a man sitting on the curb sobbing his heart out. Jesus asked him what was wrong. The man cried out in agony, "I'm a pastor!" Jesus sat down beside him, put his arm around him...and cried too.

A lot of pastors aren't laughing at that joke.

Large numbers of pastors are drinking too much and looking for love in all the wrong places. Words like *coping* and *surviving* have replaced words like *visioning* and *growing*. Dreams of Kingdom expansion are giving way to dreams of early retirement. I'm not whining, mind you. It ain't whining if it's true.

I can't get over these statistics about our fellow ministers[6]:

- 28 percent of ministers say they have at one time been forcefully terminated.

- 33 percent say that being in ministry is an outright hazard to their family.

- 75 percent report severe stress causing anguish, worry, bewilderment, anger, depression, fear, and alienation at some point in their careers.

- Doctors, lawyers, and clergy have the most problems with drug abuse, alcoholism, and suicide.

- Only 1 out of 10 local church ministers will retire from that role.

The research is both alarming and consistent.

Pastors' waistlines and blood pressures exceed the average citizen's. Certainly, some of that comes from a surprising shortage of self-discipline and a shameful lack of self-care. We've got to own that, and we'll talk about that later. But some of our health problems are undoubtedly a result of the stress of the job. So is the fact that depression is becoming a widespread curse of vocational ministry, and get this: the life expectancy of ministers is falling.[7]

We pastor-types have always had our problems. A desire to please everybody—a common trait among ministers—never has served us well. Projection onto the pastor of congregants' anger at parents or God or bad bosses also has forever been an occupational hazard. Moral failures of ministers might get more press in recent years, but they aren't new. And bullies who can't get away with intimidation at work have always found the church to be an easy place to push people around. Those issues aren't of recent origin.

Why So Hard?

I'm sure that being a spiritual leader has never been easy. But something's different nowadays. Sheri Ferguson noted that "radical changes in our society over the past 50 years have fundamentally redefined the very nature of what it means to be in ministry."[8] Why does life seem harder for ministers now? Here are some suggested reasons.

A Matter of Trust

There was a day when trust was the minister's to lose. Now it is his or hers to gain. The growing distrust of all leaders[9] makes it tough even on clergy. The proverbial pedestal might have been embarrassing and uncomfortable for ministers in the past, but it gave us a platform that we no longer have.

Incivility

Incivility is also growing in our culture, and it's infecting churches. Conflict is often cited as the number one killer of ministers' passion. Churches have always been mixed blessings to those who labor in them. Just read the New Testament; some of those churches were beyond dysfunctional. Nevertheless, Peter L. Steinke writes a lot about congregational conflict, and he declared, "Not only are the number of incidences rising, but also the number of people who are stubborn, deceptive, and mean."[10] Nastiness is rather ubiquitous. It's so bad across the pond that our British brethren are forming a ministers' union for protection against church bullies![11]

Respect under Siege

There is a universal lack of respect for authority and expertise. Physicians, for example, are being chastised and challenged by their WebMD-educated patients. Likewise, people who have a theological education and who make church leadership decisions every day are challenged on their leadership like never before by people in their congregations. Being the pastor of so many people who know best how to run the church can be exhausting!

Loyalty Decline

Institutional loyalty hasn't been popular since Nixon was President. Meaning that if your church is the Cathedral of Cool or the First Church of Perpetual Hipness, then you're in good shape. Until, that is, the Community Church of the Latest Happenin' moves down the street from you. Then those who found it easy to switch *to* your church will find it equally easy to switch *from* your church.

Stunted Growth

It's hard to make changes without the momentum that comes from growth, and church growth is rare in North America.[12] People who are otherwise resistant to new things often look around at lots of new people and are awakened to the inevitability of doing things differently.

The Youth Deficit

The growing scarcity of young adults in so many congregations makes it more difficult to make changes, and the inability to make changes makes it more difficult to reach young adults. It's another catch-22. We've got to have young adults to attract young adults, and we are not likely to reach young adults without intentional new approaches.

Secularization

The culture in North America (in fact, in much of the Northern Hemisphere) is becoming increasingly non-Christian,[13] *so attempting to grow a church is swimming against the tide.* When the church isn't growing, fingers get pointed at the ministers. In addition, when a pastor stands up before an assembly that only half fills the sanctuary, he or she is likely to deliver a half-assembly kind of sermon! Most of us are energized by the electricity that comes from a number of God's people getting together to worship and hear His word preached. When the room is not electric, the preacher is usually not electric either…which makes it less likely that people will come back to hear him or her…which makes it less likely that the preacher will preach with energy…which becomes a vicious cycle.

Elusive Relevancy

The culture is changing so rapidly that finding relevant means of communicating the unchanging story is like trying to hit a moving target. For example, if your church is just now fighting over starting a contemporary service, it's probably too late to start one. Meaningful forms of worship, as well as outreach efforts like how to "market" your church, are hard to figure out with people's routines and even worldviews changing so quickly.

The Missing Alarm

Nobody talks about sin and hell anymore![14] It is not in vogue to mention "sin" these days. "Frailties," "foibles," and "faults" are far more fashionable. And how dare a minister suggest that some people might actually spend eternity in a hopeless, Godless existence. I'm not advocating fear-based leadership, but it's significant that the congregation has lost its sense of urgency and that the role of the minister has lost some of its weight.

With this urgency gone, it has been replaced in many churches with the atmosphere of a family-friendly club. Church has commonly become a place for fun and fulfillment, group therapy, and avenues to get involved in care for our planet. We look a lot like a really good, nonthreatening, nonoffensive gathering for do-gooders. But so do lots of organizations, like your local Community Service Club, Rotary, the Sierra Club, and Girl Scouts. So, given the fact that there is not all that much difference between church and other nice organizations, and the fact that other organizations meet at more convenient times and don't ask for 10 percent of our income, why should people go to church?

In fact, it's telling that the "Atheist Churches" have become something of a phenomenon! Two British comedians were just looking for a laugh when they started the "Atheist Church," but it caught on. There is good music, a motivational message, an emphasis on righting society's wrongs, and opportunities to improve their communities. "The only thing missing," said a November 10, 2013, *USA Today* article, "is God."

I'm not suggesting we ought to try to "scare the Hell out of people." I'm just saying that the dispensing of pabulum is not serving the church well. After all, folks can go to Atheist Church for that.

The Search for Predictability

People are so frightened by the unnerving changes going on around them that they will fight for predictability in their church. Before her death, my mother was in a nursing home. While trying to care for her, I became a little frustrated with her obsession over her bedside table. She had to have every little trinket, every bottle of lotion, and every photo in a certain place. She was constantly rearranging things or asking family members to do so. I asked Keri, my wife, "What is the deal with Mom and that bedside table?"

Keri said, "Travis, that table is the only thing in her life that your mom has control over." My wife was right. All decisions, including healthcare, were being made for my mom. She couldn't even get up to go to the bathroom without waiting for her needs to fit into someone else's schedule. The only thing in life she could arrange was that bedside table. It wasn't that she was crazy or mean or had an obsessive compulsive disorder. Rather, she was scared and deeply frustrated that her world was far beyond her control.

The church has become that bedside table for some people. With so many things changing, they are determined to resist change in their church. Diana Butler Bass wrote: "People bring their fears about large-scale social change with them to church. These cultural anxieties are often a hidden source of congregational conflict." Kathleen Smith quoted Bass and then offered an example of this phenomena:

> One parishioner who was upset about changes in the order of the liturgy was confronted by his pastor as to the cause of his resistance. The older gentleman said, "Everything's changed in my life: my kids moved away, we never used to go out for lunch on Sunday and now we do...and everything else seems to be changing in my life. But by cracky, I'm not going to put up with change in church!" This man wasn't trying to start a conflict; he was trying to preserve some stability in his life.[15]

This does not excuse a prioritization of one's preferences over the needs of the congregation. It does, however, explain some of it.

So the work of the minister leading a ten-year-old church and the work of the minister leading a several-decades-old church are almost like two different professions. Church planting carries its own unique challenges, but *changing* a culture is more difficult than *creating* a culture. If you serve a church with a culture you inherited, in some ways your work is doubly difficult.

The Age Issue

Being a young minister today has unique leadership challenges. If you are a young minister, you are likely to face questions, even opposition, from all generations. Ministers under thirty are three-and-a-half times more likely than older ministers to lose their jobs because of congregational conflict.[16] Here are a few reasons why this happens.

For one, people in your generation tend to like flat organizational structures and nonhierarchical leadership. Teamwork is a priority.[17] Many in your age bracket will not like it if they perceive you to be overly fond of authority. And some in older generations will see you as too young and inexperienced to know what you're doing. Unless you are unusual, you also are going to be intimidated by people who are older and have more power, more experience, and more money.

Furthermore, until you get to be an old man or woman, some people your age are going to "compete" with you. I never thought about that until a pastor friend of mine—an unusually energetic man who served as the pastor of a large church for more than five decades—said that he noticed when he got old people didn't seem to see him as a competitor anymore. They began to see him as a father figure, and the personal digs and jabs came less frequently. Some of you have a long way to go before you become father or mother figures, although that day is sure to come.

Paul's young protégé, Timothy, could empathize with other young ministers today. He must have been facing some pushback from congregants over his youth for Paul to tell him, "Don't let anyone look down on you because you are young" (1 Tim. 4:12a). Later in that letter God inspired Paul to give Timothy specific instructions about how to lead different age groups. All that because leading a church as a young person is tricky.

So maybe it's not just paranoia. Maybe things really are harder in the church than they've ever been.

The Value of a Heads Up

I'm going to say it again. No matter your age, what you do is hard. You need to know that, and I want to affirm it. Not so you can pity yourself, but so you can have a realistic understanding of the life the Creator chose for you. Knowing this is important. I learned it the hard way many years ago.

My wife and I used to be missionaries in Nigeria, and though we eventually loved that African nation, those first few weeks were tough. Electricity and water were all too rare in that house in the ancient city of Oyo where we studied the Yoruba language. In that environment, our three-year-old daughter contracted malaria in record time. A heat rash transformed our ten-month-old into a living, breathing, scratching reminder of the torture to which we were subjecting our poor, innocent children. Language study was about as much fun as, well, language study. These trials, together with the newness of the culture, nearly propelled me past *culture shock* to *culture electrocution*.

For a month I prayed for a rare tropical disease. I wasn't suicidal; I was merely searching for an honorable way to exit. I didn't want to die; I just wanted to get sick enough to get sent home and save face.

I remember writing a letter to my mentor, Dr. Bill Cowley. Bill had been a missionary in Nigeria years earlier, and we had talked about his life there numerous times. Now, here I was wondering if I was going to make it as a missionary. In the letter I asked Bill, "Why didn't you tell me this was going to be so hard?" Knowing the answer, I still would have gone, and his warning wouldn't have made life easier. But there is something comforting about hearing someone say that what we do is hard.

I hope I am not discouraging you by telling you how hard it is to do what you do. But if you haven't discovered this yet, I want to do what I can to soften, perhaps even prevent, the surprise and shock that typically comes with that discovery. Speed Leas observed:

> A football receiver often knows he's going to be hit immediately after he makes a catch. Knowing that doesn't lessen the impact of the hit, but it does help him to hold on to the ball and sometimes even maintain his balance,

elude the tackler, and gain some extra ground. Likewise with pastors, if they know when the church is likely to be hit, they'll more likely be able to turn up-field for a few extra yards.[18]

Now, if you have already experienced how hard vocational ministry can be, I want you to know that I get it, that I have been there, that you are not alone, and that there is help and hope. So, let me say it again: What you do is hard. The call to vocational ministry often has a sharp edge to it. Spiritual leadership is both wonderful and terrible.[19]

The "B" Word

Because what you do is hard, and because you are passionate (I assume) about being an effective pastor, you are a prime candidate for *burnout.*

The majority of pastors in danger of burning out are in churches that are on a plateau or in a decline. There is a definite correlation between congregational decline and pastoral despair. On the other hand, some of you are in danger of extreme overload simply because of the growth of your church and your personal desire to reach as many people as possible. All of us who are really serious about servant leadership in Christ's Church, whatever the growth or decline of our individual congregations, are candidates for burnout.

We're losing burned-out ministers from the vocational ministry left and right. However—and it's a big *however*—"clergy" showed up as number one on *The Christian Scientist Monitor's* list of the ten happiest jobs![20] Have we an inconsistency here? Well, maybe not. When things are going well, vocational ministry really is a great life. It is a life of meaning, of contribution. It carries with it a sense of following the mission of the Creator of the universe. Vocational ministry is one of those "high risk, high rewards" deals. When it is going well, it's going really well. When it's going poorly, it's going really poorly. And it's going really poorly for a lot of ministers.

However, this is not a book griping about how awful we pastors have it. No defeatism or chips-on-the-shoulder allowed here. This is a book about hope. About faith. About choosing joy. It's about keeping at our calling. It's about loving the Church and following a biblical model for ministry. It's about the instructions given to people like you and me and recorded in Acts 20:28.

2

There and Back

"You don't need to leave the pastorate. You need to learn to be pastor differently."

—BONNIE MILLER *(my vocational counselor, when I was looking for another way to make a living)*

I have a real sensitivity to ministers who are hurting. When I hear the horror stories, my stomach literally feels ill.

Because I've been there.

I've made those hard personnel decisions when I was disparaged by people who had only faulty, secondhand information about what had happened.

I've been second-guessed by people who had neither the experience, the calling, nor the information I had.

I've also made bad calls that I lived to regret.

I've let so many balls get in the air that some dropped.

I've sat in the office of a vocational counselor, asking, "Is there another way I could make a living?"

I've survived near burnout. With help, I even found renewed joy and passion for the ministry.

If they haven't already, really hard times are probably going to come for you. I would urge you to decide now that when your crisis arises, you will not act quickly or drastically. During the crisis, you might conclude that God is calling you to another church or to another ministerial role or perhaps away from vocational ministry altogether. But please join me in a pledge now that, before you take a radical step to leave your pastoral position, you will consider if, perhaps, you can do ministry differently, in a healthier and more effective way. That's what a vocational counselor said to me when I went to her looking for another way to make a living. She eventually said, "You don't need to leave the pastorate. You need to learn to be pastor differently."

How I Almost Lost It… Then Re-found It

I had gone through years of nagging struggles. Mainly just an ongoing string of the typical frustrations: an unhappy parishioner here, a staff squabble there, an anonymous letter here, an unrealized dream there. Their constancy and occasional intensity nearly wore me out.

I made an appointment with a vocational counselor. She had me take tests to measure vocational interests. I expected this vocational counselor to tell me several places where I could go to work fairly quickly. I found out, however, that a vocational counselor is not a headhunter. Instead of pointing me to a new job, she asked (with a look of suspicion on her face), "Why exactly are you here?" She helped me realize that I was not following a divine call to another vocation; I was suffering from near burnout.

I began to read things like *Running on Empty*, by Wayne Cordeiro, and a really helpful e-book called *Pastor Pain*, by Steve Bagi. I also read Gordon McDonald's *Who Stole My Church?*, even though it wasn't touted as a book about burnout. At the end of that book, McDonald acknowledged that frustrated pastors might want to go plant a church, which is a noble endeavor. But he offered another option: staying where we are and helping our churches act like teenagers again.[1] By that McDonald meant helping churches regain their buoyancy, their passion for life, and their hope for the future. I took great encouragement from that counsel.

Then McDonald dropped a Bible verse onto a page—Acts 20:28: *"Keep watch over yourselves and all the flock of which the Holy Spirit has made you overseers. Be shepherds of the church of God, which he bought with his own blood."* Never in my Christian journey have words of Scripture arrested me like these did. I credit my present vocational ministry to those words. I internalized them. I memorized them. I scrutinized, contextualized, and personalized them. I philosophized, theologized, and sermonized over them. That verse became *my* verse. My North Star. My word from the Lord. I decided I wouldn't quit. Rather, I would live Acts 20:28.

And that I did. Still, about a year later I almost relapsed. It was one of those ministerial train wrecks that some don't survive. It was one of those "God don't let it happen to me" staff issues that I had to deal with as the pastor. There was no "right" way for me to handle it, and there were plenty of "wrong" ways. I got good counsel and handled the situation the best I knew how.

It didn't go well. The church lost a few good folks. I was called a hypocrite for preaching grace and doling out judgment. My judgment was openly questioned by folks who didn't know the back story. And, worst of all, I almost lost some of the church staff. They didn't turn *on* me; they turned *from* me. At least a few. It was hard for them to trust me, for I learned that up to that point they didn't really feel like they *knew* me. I would have bet you a hundred bucks that every staff member would follow me even through the fire. But I looked around, and they weren't there. I didn't blame them, mind you. I hadn't sufficiently nurtured my relationship with them. When I said, "Come on, you know me; trust me," what I got was, "Well, we don't really know you because you don't share your heart with us very often."

On that Friday afternoon of probably the toughest week of my ministry, two friends sat in my den with me while I had something of a meltdown. My wife Keri called from her office to check on me. I couldn't get any words out. She recognized my anguish. "I'll be right there," she said.

"You need to see Dan Elash, and you need to see him immediately," one of my friends told me while we sat there waiting for me to pull myself together. I took his counsel.

On the following Monday afternoon, I was sitting at Panera Bread with Dan, pouring my heart out and soaking up his advice. A wise executive coach, he advised me for the next fourteen months. His help was invaluable. He interviewed staff members and laypersons, and then coached me on how to lead based on what he was hearing.

Perhaps his most important counsel had a connection to one of my hobbies—refereeing high school football. As a referee, my role is to run a fair, safe game, not to concern myself with the input of coaches and players. (And we get lots of "input," especially from coaches.) As a referee, my interest is not the feelings of the coaches, players, or even fellow officials; my interest is in the game itself. A referee is somewhat detached—a decision-maker, not a life coach.

Dan said that's how I was leading the staff—like a referee! So he taught me to be more self-revealing, more vulnerable, more caring, and more personal.

I'm afraid that if I hadn't suffered that crisis, I wouldn't have changed. I came to realize that image management was not going to cut it. I had to think, serve, and lead differently. After that near crisis, our staff relations became much better.

So *getting help* was the first of three things that got me through that crisis. Dan's role was critical. So was that provided by Maurice Graham, a therapist who specializes in ministers. Maurice is a great friend who often listens and advises. So I got good help from trained, experienced people.

Equally important was the friendship of a few close minister-friends. I can't say enough about those guys, and I can't stress enough the importance of intentionally establishing friendships. They are so much fun in the good times, and they are critical in the hard times. I hope you have a couple of friends like that. If not, you need to make some—the sooner, the better.

The second thing that got me through that personal train wreck was *the voice of God*. Yes, the voice of God. I'm not kidding. And it came through Chris Backert, a young Christian leader to whom I refer as my "reverse mentor." He is a deeply spiritual young man who helps me understand his generation. He also chose to be a really good friend to me.

Chris knew I was hurting, and he asked to meet me at a nearby river to pray. We met at a picturesque spot on the James River called the "Pony Pasture." (I still have a scar on my left knee as a memento of that morning. Chris turned out to be more agile than I was while crossing slick rocks.) We had talked a while when Chris said, "I think I have a word from the Lord for you."

Let me pause for a moment and tell you something about Chris. On three occasions I have heard Chris hesitate before a sentence and say something like, "I believe these next words are from the Lord." I believe they indeed have been, and each time they have been a great blessing.

"I think I have a word from the Lord for you," Chris said. "God is going to say to you, 'My grace is sufficient for you.'"

"That's it?" I asked Chris. I expected something a little more dramatically prophetic.

But that was it.

So I started listening for the words. I kept expecting God to whisper, perhaps audibly, "My grace is sufficient for you." Nothing.

Chris would e-mail, call, or text, and I'd always report, "He's not told me yet."

Then weeks later, on a Sunday morning, David Bailey was leading worship in one of our services. David is a great gift from God to the church where I was the pastor, and this particular morning was his first Sunday with us. God's Spirit seemed to be blessing us with an unusual awareness of His presence that morning. It was one of those rare, mountaintop experiences.

I had my eyes closed, though I don't often do that. I had stopped singing and was just enjoying the worship. I was unaware even of the song we were singing; it just wasn't registering. I was carried away by the sense of what was happening in the room.

Then I opened my eyes. At that moment, for the first time, I realized the song that the congregation was singing: *"Your grace is enough. Your grace is enough. Your grace is enough for me."* I began to weep…to the point that I began to worry I would be unable to compose myself before I had to stand to speak in a few minutes. I was simply overwhelmed. God whispered clearly to me, "This is my message to you."

I texted Chris Backert immediately after the service. "God told me today," I wrote.

I look back now and marvel at how God set that up. He'd been biding His time, orchestrating everything: from David's coming to our church to the choice of that song. And the Creator of the universe, the One who spoke the universe into being, finally whispered to my spirit, "My grace is enough for you."[2]

The third thing that got me through the crisis was *Acts 20:28*. Again. This text returned as God's word directly to me: "Keep watch over yourselves and all the flock of which the Holy Spirit has made you overseers. Be shepherds of the church of God, which he bought with his own blood." For a second time Acts 20:28 was my salvation.

Getting help, hearing from God, and Acts 20:28 saw me through my brush with burnout. For years afterward, I remained a local church pastor. I kept leading our church staff and congregation. Troubles, struggles, and frustrations still came, as they do for any minister, but I kept getting healthier, wiser (I hope), and more taken up with substance. Being a pastor, frankly, became a lot more fun. I pastored differently because I became a different man, a restored and transformed leader—in Christ, and through his grace.

Years after these defining crises, I left the pastorate. In 2014, after thirty years as a pastor and missionary, I accepted a position with *Fresh Expressions US* to help congregations like the ones I've served figure out new forms of church for people who never are going to be reached by more conventional means. I also began to consult with churches—helping with transitions, conflict, vision, and mission strategies. That combination role is the culmination of all the experiences I've had as a missionary and pastor, together with my academic preparation in the area of cross-cultural missions. I followed my passions and skills and a sense of divine call that took me from the local church to a ministry that has me helping congregations and ministers be healthy and missional.

The important thing here is that, after my near collapse into burnout, I'd become healthy enough to make a good decision. I was years beyond my lowest point when I assumed my present role, and I was able to make a sound decision in response to the Spirit's prompting. I wasn't looking to leave pastoral ministry due to some stressor. Rather, I was spiritually and psychologically well—in the condition I needed to be to move on in a healthy way, if that was what God wanted me to do. I was able to enjoy the role of pastor, enjoy years of fruitfulness, and then respond prayerfully and deliberately, not react impulsively, to the new call when it came. My ability to make a calm and confident decision came largely from the work of the Spirit via Acts 20:28.

Acts 20:28 will be our map for the rest of this book. Let me tell you the story of those words from God through the apostle Paul.

Acts 20:28 and Its Setting

The apostle Paul had called together the elders from around Ephesus for a last "goodbye." He was on his way to Jerusalem where it was assumed he would make his last stand. They were more than partners, these men and Paul. They were colleagues, fellow pioneers, comrades. It was a tender scene. Paul's friends pleaded with him not to take the risk to travel back to Jerusalem. Yet Paul explained that he was "compelled by the Spirit" to go there, admitting he'd probably never see them again. Paul knew his friends' ongoing pastoral work would be difficult. He knew they would face opposition from inside and outside, and that "friendly fire" would hurt the most. But he knew what he needed to do, and that involved leaving these Christian leaders behind as he set his face for the Holy City. So he used his last moments with them to summarize what a healthy, biblical ministry looks like.

I know those words were spoken two millennia ago, and to people in a far different world from our own. Yet those words feel very personal. That is why I found the story behind those words so captivating.

A Discovery at Qumran

One of the most fascinating experiences of my sabbatical studies in Israel a few years ago was the morning our class spent at Qumran. When that shepherd boy in 1946 stumbled on all that old papyrus in those caves near the Dead Sea, he made quite a stir. Biblical scholars got as worked up as European soccer fans.

A discovery, though, that got little press was a letter from one known only as Joseph, a pastor living in Miletus around 90 A.D. A Qumran scroll containing his letter to the congregation he served got left on the bottom of the pile while scholars poured over fragments of New Testament letters. Never has this letter gotten the attention that I believe it deserves. Scholars studying this letter have concluded that pastor, Joseph, was present the day when Paul called the Ephesian elders together, as Luke recorded in Acts 20.

Here is the passage from Joseph's writings that I find most intriguing:

> Brothers, I do not boast regarding the leadership to which God has appointed me. A place of service in the house of God is a gift of God's mercy. Yet, Brothers, it has come to my attention that there are many who believe the common calling shared by all believers negates the particular calling to oversight in his church. It is deeply distressing, my dear friends, to have people in the household of God, including those of the family of Jonathan, who remain on the milk of the word, who seem intent on opposing my spiritual leadership. Our overseer and apostle, Paul, has proved to be prophetic on this matter.
>
> I have declared the full counsel of God without fear beyond the congregation of faith. While the good news

of the Christ is not always welcomed, it appears that the greatest opposition to my ministry is from within the church. This, my brothers, is very disheartening. While my commitment is to the entire body of Christ, I confess my struggles with some. The church of God is the gift of the blood of our Lord, Jesus, and I long to be able to give my whole heart to her. I long to escape the narrow and critical murmuring that seems to come with the office of pastor. Some of my fellow servants already have returned to worldly vocations and I do confess the temptation to do the same.

What an incredible letter! If only it had been real. I confess I made up that whole discovery-from-Qumran story. There was no letter from a pastor named Joseph in Miletus. Not that I know of, anyway. But there certainly *could* have been. The laments of this fictitious letter relate struggles that have been repeated countless times by pastors since the first century. People who have no business doing so have questioned the spiritual authority of ministers serving at God's command. Innumerable people have crippled the congregations of which they counted themselves members. And I'd venture that every person ever to hold church office has longed to escape the narrow and critical murmuring that seems so pervasive.

Ministers? Elders?

I am certain those in the original gathering described in Acts 20 long remembered the words of Paul. When they were wondering if they should return to fishing or tailoring or trading or whatever they were doing before they became pastors, I'm certain God brought Paul's declaration to their minds. Because what they did was hard.

I pray God will call those words of Acts 20:28 to your mind, too, when you are slogging through a particularly difficult stretch of ministry. Those words are instructive no matter your title or role in vocational ministry.

Now, the men to whom Paul was speaking were called "elders," and I owe you a word of explanation about my interpretation of the roles held by those men to whom Paul spoke in Acts 20:28. Acts 20:17 says that Paul had "sent for the elders of the church." Luke used the term *presbyterous* (elders) there. Yet, when Paul spoke of that group, he also used the words that we are focusing on here: "overseers" (*episkopous,* bishops) and "shepherds" (*poimainein,* "pastors"). Given these usages, I believe these three terms—elder, overseer, and pastor—were interchangeable and synonymous terms for Paul. Church structure was still under development in the mid first century. The church offices that we now know were simply not defined when Paul offered his counsel to the congregational leaders in Ephesus.[3]

So in the pages that follow, I will be assuming that what Paul said is applicable to you and to all vocational ministers—all those who are called by God to serve as spiritual leaders, particularly in local churches.[4]

3

Keep Watch

"Keep watch over yourselves..."

"The people of God are always in a struggle with the agenda issue. They are like the lighthouse keeper who was given a specified amount of fuel each month with which to light his beacon. His job was to use it judiciously and to make certain there was enough available for an emergency. One day a fisherman, having run out of fuel in his boat, came and asked for a little fuel so he could complete his journey to the shore, and, of course, the lighthouse keeper complied. He was followed by an excursion boat taking tourists to see the deep waters and to appreciate the beautiful shoreline. He found himself in the same predicament, and so to help the people, he gave away some of the precious fuel. Several weeks later a party boat came, filled with revelers. The captain had not made provision, so the keeper gave away some more of the precious fuel to help these people also. Finally, on a dark and stormy night, the light was needed, but the keeper had no fuel for the light. Lives were lost unnecessarily."

—BILL SELF, IN *DEFINING MOMENTS*[1]

Acts 20:28 not only changed me and my pastoral ministry, it still shapes and guides my new role with *Fresh Expressions US* and as a consultant to churches and pastors. In my new roles I have conversations with multiple congregations and ministers every week. And the more I learn, the more I realize how hard vocational ministry is no matter where it takes place and how badly the Church needs good, servant leaders who are living out a biblical model for that ministry.

My heart still beats for pastors. In fact, I now have an even greater passion for fellow vocational ministers. When I hear another story of an embattled pastor or church staff member (and I hear those stories increasingly often), I literally have a visceral reaction. In days gone by when I heard about a minister under pressure, I'd think, "Bummer." Now those accounts create a sick feeling in my stomach.

I am not a disinterested academician speaking to you. I write as one whose pain is a clear memory. Yet I write as one who is now healthy, strong, and confident, and as one who hurts for those who have not secured those benefits yet and may even wonder if they are attainable. And let me repeat: you do not have to leave the pastorate or your present position to have what I'm talking about. I found that out in my pastoral work, and you can too.

So let's start digging into the biblical passage that I believe provides the key to opening a new, healthier way to church ministry. We'll begin by reading through the story in which Acts 20:28 is couched:

> From Miletus, Paul sent to Ephesus for the elders of the church. When they arrived, he said to them: "You know how I lived the whole time I was with you, from the first day I came into the province of Asia. I served the Lord with great humility and with tears, and in the midst of severe testing by the plots of my Jewish opponents. You know that I have not hesitated to preach anything that would be helpful to you but have taught you publicly and from house to house. I have declared to both Jews and Greeks that they must turn to God and have faith in our Lord Jesus.
>
> " And now, as a captive to the Spirit, I am going to Jerusalem, not knowing what will happen to me there. I only know that in every city the Holy Spirit warns me that prison and hardships are facing me. However, I consider my life worth nothing to me; my only aim is to finish the race and complete the task the Lord Jesus has given me—the task of testifying to the good news of God's grace.

"Now I know that none of you among whom I have gone about preaching the kingdom will ever see me again. Therefore, I declare to you today that I am innocent of the blood of any of you. For I have not hesitated to proclaim to you the whole will of God. *Keep watch over yourselves and all the flock, of which the Holy Spirit has made you overseers. Be shepherds of the church of God, which he bought with his own bloo*d. Know that after I leave, savage wolves will come in among you and will not spare the flock. Even from your own number men will arise and distort the truth in order to draw away disciples after them. So be on your guard! Remember that for three years I never stopped warning each of you night and day with tears.

"Now I commit you to God and to the word of his grace, which can build you up and give you an inheritance among all those who are sanctified. I have not coveted anyone's silver or gold or clothing. You yourselves know that these hands of mine have supplied my own needs and the needs of my companions. In everything I did, I showed you that by this kind of hard work we must help the weak, remembering the words the Lord Jesus himself said: 'It is more blessed to give than to receive.' "

When Paul had finished speaking, he knelt down with all of them and prayed. They all wept as they embraced him and kissed him. What grieved them most was his statement that they would never see his face again. Then they accompanied him to the ship. (Acts 20:17–38, emphasis added)

I italicized verse 28 because this is the advice Paul gave that I want to explore, explain, and apply. Notice that he gives this counsel out of his own ministry experience in what we know today as Asia Minor. And he served "with great humility and with tears," enduring "severe testing" and "plots." His work came with pain and struggle and hardship. Out of this crucible came his counsel to ministers in verse 28: *"Keep watch over yourselves and over all the flock, of which the Holy Spirit has made you overseers. Be shepherds of the church of God, which he bought with his own blood."*

Let's dig into Paul's advice to us, starting where he starts: "Keep watch over yourselves." The *Amplified Bible* translates it like this:

"Take care and be on guard for yourselves." In the *English Standard Version* it reads, "Pay careful attention to yourselves." According to New Testament commentator William Barclay, the first part of Acts 20:28 should read, "Take heed for yourselves and take heed for all the flock."[2]

"Keep watch over" is a translation of the Greek word *prosexo*. According to *Bauer's* Greek lexicon, *prosexo* means "Turn one's mind to…pay attention to, give heed to, pay attention, be alert, notice…be concerned about, care for…occupy oneself with, devote or apply oneself…"[3]

A century ago, missiologist and Bible scholar W. O. Carver offered this commentary on verse 28: "They need to take heed ('look out for') themselves and for all the flock. To Timothy, Paul writes, 'Take heed to thyself and to thy teaching' (1 Timothy 4:15). Not, of course, look out for their own interest, but watch against defects and failures in themselves."[4] This reminds me of the instructions at the beginning of a flight about the oxygen masks. "If the oxygen masks fall from the panels above because of a change in the cabin pressure," we are told, "first secure your own mask before assisting others." The obvious message is that if you are deprived of oxygen, you are of little use to the one next to you. Likewise, the evidence surrounding Acts 20:28 seems clear: Our chief and first responsibility as spiritual leaders is to lead ourselves. Greek language resources leave no doubt in my mind that it was intentional—certainly divinely inspired—that the first instruction to these ministers was to pay attention to themselves. That includes, as Carver noted, for ministers to pay attention to their "defects and failures." In other words, the road to ministerial health begins with a close, honest look at ourselves. And that's where we will start.

The Church's Health and Our Health

Years ago I bought a copy of Peter Scazerro's *The Emotionally Healthy Church* because I wanted the church I served as pastor to be emotionally healthy. I was surprised (and, I admit, a little disappointed) to find that the book is mainly about the health of the church's *leaders*. Yet Scazerro is right: the health of our congregations depends largely on *our* health. We ministers have to take a step back and engage in self-evaluation—even to "watch against defects and failures" in ourselves. For when there are problems in our churches, many of us tend to assume others are to blame.

It's simply not helpful for ministers to carp about how uncooperative and inflexible our congregations are, for example, unless we are simultaneously admitting our ineptness at navigating change. I am not sympathetic when I hear ministers who've been terminated demonize the congregation without also owning up to their own contributions to the painful situation. Rare is the minister who is a completely innocent party in a church brouhaha. We are often part of the problem.

The truth is, some vocational ministers have significant issues. From narcissism to neuroses. From quirks to psychoses. From immaturity to immorality. From social awkwardness to spiritual childishness. From a penchant for faux pas to a penchant for hissy fits.

If there is a dysfunction in the church, it might be centered in the church office.

Not every criticism of us is valid, of course. However, in my case at least, I have to admit that a good dose of the criticism that has come *my* way over the years has been warranted. And my relationships with multiple churches and ministers since I left the pastorate have made it clear that my experience was not unique but more common than many ministers are willing to admit.

I love ministers, and I don't mean to bash members of the ministerial fraternity. I simply want to warn all of us against automatically jumping to the conclusion that we are innocent victims of ruthless congregations. Some of us who are in trouble at our churches haven't "kept watch over" ourselves. We are not always the guiltless prey of cold-hearted troublemakers.

Occasionally, of course, there really are the pure-hearted ministers who get knocked around by ruthless sociopaths. I know some of those stories. There are some really unhealthy, terribly unhappy, downright ungodly people in church pews; we will talk about them later on. It is unproductive, however, to assume too quickly that we are the blameless casualties of church wars.

Often our contribution to church troubles is more passive than active; we unintentionally make the congregation susceptible to disease by not taking care of ourselves. It's not that we always directly kindle conflict. Sometimes unrest spreads within the congregation simply because we ministers do not have the emotional, physical, or spiritual wherewithal to deal with even marginal dissonance in a productive way. More times than we'd like to admit, our personal and congregational problems are somehow traceable to our own lack of emotional, physical, or spiritual health. And most of us, most of the time, are about as healthy as we choose to be. Unfortunately, when we do not make a conscious effort at being our best, the well-being and mission of our churches suffer.

"When the bucket's empty, everything scrapes the bottom." I recently heard a pastor friend use those words to communicate the truth that, when we are emotionally spent, most any frustration becomes a major issue. So someone says something we don't like, or a church vote doesn't go our way, or the car won't start…and suddenly we are saying something we will soon regret, drafting a resignation letter, or at least updating our resumes. We've got to keep water in our buckets.

But this doesn't happen by accident. Buckets don't fill themselves. And most of us do not reach out for the help we need when our water gets low or completely evaporates. We simply must assume more responsibility for our health. And the quest for health is multi-faceted, so let's talk about comprehensive, all-inclusive, across-the-board health.

Keep Watch over Your Emotional Health

One of the hardest things a minister can do is admit that he or she is hurting.

Years ago I was sobered when I read a story in *USA Today* about a forty-two-year-old North Carolina pastor who took his life. Greg Warner, the article's author, wrote:

> What kind of personal pain would cause a 42-year-old pastor to abandon his family, his calling and even life itself? Members of a Baptist church here are asking that question after their pastor committed suicide in his parked car in September.
>
> Those who counsel pastors say Christian culture, especially Southern evangelicalism, creates the perfect environment for depression. Pastors suffer in silence,

unwilling or unable to seek help or even talk about it. Sometimes they leave the ministry. Occasionally the result is the unthinkable.[5]

It is hard for ministers to admit personal pain, whether we're Southern evangelicals or not. But admit it we must, and sometimes to our congregations.

One Sunday morning the wife of one of my pastor friends took her husband's place in the pulpit. She explained that their pastor, her husband, wasn't present that morning because he was in the hospital being treated for depression. My friend feared that announcing his depression would be the end of his pastorate, but it actually became something of a new beginning. People rallied around him. Folks came out of the woodwork to express how grateful they were that their pastor would acknowledge an illness that had haunted them, too. My friend is healthy today, and so is his church, largely because he was honest about his depression.

So, if depression ever does visit you, please admit it to yourself and to people who can help you. There are some really good places for hurting ministers to get help. You probably can Google your way to several local sources of solace. Wherever you get help, please get it.

Often, however, depression will not be the problem we face. Instead it will be an inner turmoil that is less dramatic, less obvious. We'll experience an indefinable restlessness, an indescribable melancholy—that mysterious feeling that comes and goes. It may feel as if you have a softball stuck in your gut. That condition is burnout, or something rubbing up against it.

Burnout is described in several ways. Because I came so close to experiencing it, I've tried to understand this phenomenon that robs so many of fruitful ministry. Here is what I have learned about it. Burnout is…

- **Fatigue.** I'm talking about a deep weariness. Lethargy. When I was nearing burnout, I remember saying to several people, "I'm tired, so tired."

- **Disillusionment.** Disillusionment is the sense that we're not making a difference. Ministers who are disillusioned say things like, "I'm just keeping the machine running. I'm spinning my wheels." When I was nearing burnout myself,

I wondered if anything of real significance was happening. I couldn't see what God was doing.

- **Cynicism.** Disillusionment can quickly turn into cynicism. All the things wrong with the church can eclipse the many things right with the church. When the burned out minister thinks of his or her congregation, it's the faces of the curmudgeons, not the saints, who come to mind.

- **Withdrawal.** It becomes easier not to be present, either emotionally or even physically. Personally, at my low point, I would sneak out the back door after worship services so I could avoid passing through the halls and lobby where I'd have to talk to people.

- **Disconnect.** Burnout is a big, fat disconnect. This is how former pastor Daniel Sherman describes it, quoting Michael Leiter and Christina Maslach: "Burnout is a gradual process of loss during which the mismatch between the needs of the person and the demands of the job grows even greater." Then Sherman continues: "No one likes every aspect of their job. There are no perfect matches… But as burnout slowly creeps into your life, the mismatches begin to deepen and new mismatches start to appear."[6]

- **Relational drought.** The cause of burnout is usually more about bad relationships than about an overly demanding workload. Most of us can work hard if we are doing things we love and believe in. In fact, some of us work *too hard* at those things. But when there is an abundance of personal conflicts and a dearth of fun and friendships, burnout is a real hazard.

- **Cumulative.** Burnout is rarely a sudden occurrence. It comes on gradually, often imperceptibly. It involves the piling up of miniature resentments, slight regrets, and trivial annoyances, usually combined with a couple of full-blown calamities.

I am acquainted with all the above, and my writing about burnout is cathartic. I've been there and back, and I write with a prayer and hope that something you find here will enable you to recognize it, avoid it, or, at least, by God's grace, live to tell the tale about it.

Some Counsel for Emotional Well-Being

Remember when I told you about my visits with the vocational counselor? She told me, "You don't need to leave the pastorate. You need to learn to be pastor differently." That's how, I believe, we protect ourselves against burning out. We learn how to do ministry differently. For example...

Do less of what is incongruent with who you are. In pastoral ministry, we often find ourselves in a mismatch between our gifts and the things our roles require us to do. If this gulf is too wide, or we find ourselves too often on the side of the gulf where our weaknesses and inadequacies loom large and frustrate our best efforts, we might despair over the role to which we believe God called us. We might even question our calling. This is where resentment and depression can set in.

Rather than falling into that trap, take stock of who you are, your spiritual gifts, and natural talents. As much as is possible in your setting, let your roles be defined by how God shaped you. Explain to your church leaders your assessment of who God created you to be and what you believe would be the fulfillment of God's calling for you. See if they would be willing to renegotiate your role so that it is more compatible with your giftedness. Of course, you will want to be reasonable; there might be some tasks that simply are necessary whether or not you feel they "fit." Still, I encourage you to speak with those who make the decisions about your job description. Tell them you want them to have the best you were created by God to offer. Let 1 Timothy 4:14–15 be your guide and support for that conversation: "Do not neglect your gift, which was given you through a prophecy when the body of elders laid their hands on you. Be diligent in these matters; give yourself wholly to them, so that everyone may see your progress."

If you are running around trying to fulfill all the expectations that others have of you, you might neglect your gift—that thing God called you and only you to do. So stop now and think: *What could I give up and hand off to someone else? Do I really need to teach that class or be the church's primary counselor? Can't someone else do this or that?* Let your leaders help you establish priorities that serve both you and the church well. Leadership consultant Richard Kriegbaum suggests that "real weariness comes not from working long and hard but from attempting something for which I am not well suited or trying more than God made me capable of doing."[7]

You and I were never meant to try the impossible, much less be held accountable for it. So be honest with yourself about what you do well, about what you could do better if you were to work on it, and about what you simply were not created to do. Work with your leaders to build on your strengths and to see where others on the team could compensate for your limitations. (Those others on the team might like a renegotiation of their roles, too!) Your effectiveness and joy in ministry will grow exponentially.

Go home earlier. That is one of the biggest and most helpful changes I made in my last several years as a pastor. I used to stay late in the office, even if I began the day with a 7:00 a.m. breakfast meeting. Or, if I had an evening meeting at the church building, I'd just stay at the office and go home even later at night. I finally wised up. If I had an unusually early start or if I had a long evening meeting coming up, I'd almost always be gone by or before 4:30 p.m. That one adjustment made a world of difference for me. I felt like I was getting a little mini-vacation at the end of the day.

Watch your schedule. Especially during the tough stretches. When the church is clicking on all cylinders—when the vision is clear and the fellowship is sweet and the machinery is humming and the Spirit's blessing is evident—I could work long hours and still be energized. However, when there was tension in the air, when relationships were strained, when the vision was being debated… I imposed reasonable restrictions on my work hours. All of us need rest and play. Hard work is admirable, but incessant work is not. Go home. Get some rest. Rejuvenate. You will be better for it, and those around you will enjoy you more!

Get a circle of friends. Being a minister can be terribly lonely. One of our own said, "No one told me just how lonely it can be being a pastor…Maybe it's different as people don't see you as regular folks. Maybe it's because we couldn't just pack up and go away with the crowd on weekends. Maybe it's because everyone assumes that you have a lot of friends and so they don't make the move."[8] Whatever the reason, loneliness is perhaps a minister's worst yet most constant companion.

I once complained to my wife that I didn't have any close friends. My sympathetic spouse answered, "Well, it's your fault!"

So I went out and made some. I can't tell you how important that has become to me. You know the old saying: "If you want a friend, you've gotta *be* a friend." Being a friend to someone is one of the very best things you can do to ensure your emotional health.

So if you have a good friend, grab a cup of coffee with him or her and talk about your feelings, your struggles. As frightening as that might sound, you'll be better for it.

Establish a circle of lay ministry partners. One of the best things I did during a particularly rough patch was to form an informal advisory group. I didn't ask permission from the church, for I was not forming a committee to take formal action. I just needed a circle of high-capacity advisors—folks who understood the church and who loved me. We called it the "Saturday Group," since we met at 7:00 a.m. one Saturday per month. I found great strength in the mere communication of information with them, especially information about potentially controversial issues. It felt a bit like sharing the burden. Furthermore, disseminating important information throughout the church via the concentric circles—with those guys being the first circle—was an effective strategy in educating our great congregation on crucial matters.

My nature is to charge the hill, alone if need be. I learned that it is much better to be surrounded by shield-bearing friends during the charge, and those guys in the Saturday group surrounded me. I also learned that I didn't always have to be the first one to the hill. I didn't, in other words, always have to be the one standing in front of the congregation saying, "This is the way, go ye in it!" I was glad to have those guys challenging me when I needed it and standing beside me when I needed it.

Establish a forum for wrestling with divisive matters. Somewhere along the way, I read that church members and ministers need a place (besides the phone, e-mail, or the parking lot) to air their concerns about potentially divisive church problems. So at our church we formed the Matthew 18 Team, a sub-set of our deacons. If there was a difficult church issue, then people could go to the Matthew 18 Team for answers or mediation.

In that congregation, deacons were charged with keeping the unity of the spirit. So in keeping with the mission/purpose of our deacon body, the deacons formed a Matthew 18 Team that was available to hear concerns from the members of the church family. The Matthew 18 Team had the charge to address those concerns in a way that would maintain unity and spiritual health within the congregation. It wasn't used as often as I would have liked, but when people took advantage of it, it worked beautifully to address the members' concerns and to prevent hostilities.

What can you establish in your church setting that can help navigate divisive terrain and maintain church unity?

Don't join the staff of a church with a history of splittin' and spittin'. One way to take care of yourself is to avoid churches that have a reputation for wounding their ministers. Many are the churches with a track record of splitting up and spitting out ministers. In fact, according to one national study of churches, "[S] even percent of congregations accounted for more than 35 percent of all the conflict."[9] Spare yourself and stay away from them.

I know of and have heard of lots of pastors who have been aware of the horror stories surrounding a church's ministerial casualties yet thought they would be the ones to change things. I understand that people sometimes sense that God truly has called them to those difficult congregations. But God should send you an e-mail and a tweet and maybe even a FedEx package with explicit instructions before you decide to be the one to turn back the tide.

Guy Greenfield was one of those ministers who thought things would be different for him. Oh, he knew that "over a period of twenty-five years, this church had had seven ministers, not one of whom had had a pleasant exit." Yet he decided to serve that congregation and be the one to rescue them. Then, after two years, Greenfield had decided, "I was not Jesus. This church was not worth dying for."[10]

Some congregations are simply toxic. They don't need another pastor to sacrifice, so please don't offer yourself on their altar.

Check your unhealthy ambition, or whatever your "dark side" is. Years ago I read Robert Schnase's book *Ambition in Ministry: Our Struggle with Success, Achievement, and Competition.* Schnase applauds the passion for expanding God's Kingdom, yet he cautions us to be vigilant regarding our potential for self-aggrandizement.

I certainly have a propensity for selfish ambition. From Schnase I learned—and still am learning—to ride herd on it. I am learning to be content with God's grace—His unconditional, undeserved, unlimited, unrelenting love. I am learning to be glad for the success of others. I am learning to define effectiveness by means other than the number of people who attend the services in which I preach or read the books that I write. I am learning that my value is not in my performance.

Another important book for me has been *Overcoming the Dark Side of Leadership: How to Become an Effective Leader by Confronting Potential Failures,* by Gary L. McIntosh and Samuel D. Rima. McIntosh and Rima helped me understand that there is a soft and dangerous underbelly to the very personal traits that I would say are my strengths. We all have them—personal dysfunctions— the dark sides to our personalities. McIntosh and Rima warn of the dangers to ourselves and our congregations that our dark sides pose. The authors counsel us to wrestle with those dark sides, such as narcissism, paranoia, codependence, and passive aggressiveness—to "ride the monsters all the way down,"[11] even if it's painful.

Be honest with yourself. And when you identify those troubling sides to yourself, don't suppress or ignore them. Deal with them. Reading books such as the ones just mentioned are good places to start.

Self-differentiate. If you are not aware of the term *self-differentiation,* you need more orientation than I can offer here.[12] I suggest you study the concept in the writings of Murray Bowen, Edwin Friedman, and the like.[13] Here, let me say simply that self-differentiation allows one to value relationships without being dependent upon those relationships for a sense of self-value and well-being. Self-differentiation encourages objectivity and a "non-anxious presence," even in tough conversations. The desire to either conform or control is minimized so that we can function in a way that is healthy for ourselves and the system we are in. Self-differentiated people are comfortable defining themselves and in affirming differing approaches. Self-differentiated people are consistent and trustworthy, even if their opinions are not always embraced by the group.

When applied to ecclesiastical settings, it means a self-differentiated congregational leader understands the dynamics of the church, even the dynamics of individual teams or committees, and he or she functions in a healthy way within those dynamics. Neither dependent upon affirmation nor deflated by rejection, he or she can be who God created him or her to be without either cowering or bullying. It turns out your mom was right when she told you to just "be yourself." Perhaps without realizing it, she was affirming the importance of self-differentiation.

Your emotional condition will not go unnoticed by the people you serve. I always have thought I could bluff pretty well—that I could put on a pastoral smile and fake my way through anything. I've been absolutely shocked at how many times people have said to me during one of my emotional dips, "You look tired," or, "You look troubled." Or they have asked, "Are you okay?" I could have sworn I was acting as jovial as ever, but people picked up on my mood. And they did it almost every time. It's hard to hide an anxious heart.

Keep Watch Over Your *Spiritual* Health

Wayne Cordeiro—pastor, speaker, author, and songwriter— tells about his personal bout with burnout in his book *Leading on Empty.* There he reminds us how important it is to invest in our souls *now*:

> During this winter season, the only things I had to hold onto were the disciplines I had *already built* into my life. In the night, a sailor cannot see land, nor can he get his bearings from the coastline. He must navigate by trusting the dimly lit buoys already set in place. In the same way, when you go through dark seasons, you will be restricted by, or released to, what has already been established within your soul.[14]

I encourage you to prepare for the inevitable crises of ministry by engaging in the spiritual disciplines now. Study scripture. Practice solitude. Fast. Worship; really worship. Become a person of prayer. Serve in ways that are outside your professional role. Read established authors on the spiritual disciplines, such as Dallas Willard, Richard Foster, and James Bryan Smith. Take the time to learn to practice the disciplines that best "renovate your heart."

Richard Foster said, "The desperate need today is not for a great number of intelligent people, or gifted people, but for deep people."[15] When it comes to ministers and Christian mentors,

I believe the average Christ-follower today is not looking for a spiritual *leader,* but rather for a *spiritual* leader. There is a hunger for the kind of depth that borders on the mysteriously mystical. People want to believe that the person pointing the way actually travels the way.

Have you ever yelled down into a deep well and heard the echo that says, "This is a big place down here—bigger than you can see from where you stand"? People long for the kind of leader from whom there rings just such an echo.

You can be a *spiritual* leader, but it will take work. The work of the disciplines. As Gordon MacDonald wrote, "Spirituality has its price."[16]

I don't give this counsel lightly. I understand that vocational ministry can both encourage and discourage our spiritual lives. On the one hand, I understand what Barbara Brown Taylor said in her book *Leaving Church*: "My role and my soul were eating each other alive."[17] I know a minister who retired early and said to me, "I had to get out of the ministry while I was still a Christian!" I get that. At times I, too, felt like vocational ministry was taking its toll on my spirituality. On the other hand, I fully identify with the declaration of Martin B. Copenhavor: "Being a pastor has made me better than I am."[18] I get this too, because mainly I felt like I was a better Christ-follower because of my calling to the local church. I admit that sometimes I did my personal devotional reading, initiated spiritual conversations with people who were far from God, cared for widows and orphans, and prioritized my family because I needed to be a good example to the congregation and because I was *supposed* to do that kind of thing as a pastor. Yet, I also found that by actually doing those things—even if I did them *because* I was a pastor—I changed for the better.

So let's embrace the role of minister and celebrate the fact that we actually have a little extra motivation, and perhaps a few extra resources, for living the Christian life. Let's acknowledge that we really have no excuse for not keeping watch over our spiritual health.

While we're considering the topic of spiritual health, by the way, there might be no more critical question than this: "How much do I love Jesus?" When it comes to keeping watch over ourselves, I'm convinced this is the fundamental question: Do I really love Jesus? Am I doing his will the best I understand it? Am I living my life as he would live my life? And, candidly, Does my heart warm with the thought of him?

You know the story: Three times Jesus asked, "Do you love me?" Well, do you?

One of the most meaningful paragraphs I have ever read is in Henri Nouwen's book *In the Name of Jesus: Reflections on Christian Leadership*. I read the book because I read a lot about leadership. I am fascinated by great leaders. And I will be honest—along with all the frustrations of leadership, there also is something pretty heady, invigorating, and intoxicating about leadership. But the most important words I have read about leadership are Nouwen's: "The question is not: How many people take you seriously? How much are you going to accomplish? Can you show some results? But: Are you in love with Jesus?"[19] That is the ultimate question for spiritual leadership and absolutely one of the key questions of life. "Do you love Jesus?" This question still demands an answer from those of us entrusted to shepherd his sheep.

Keep Watch over Your *Intellectual* Health

If you want to be a servant-leader, or a better servant-leader, then never stop learning.

NBA referee Joey Crawford stated, "Say I'm the crew chief on a game and we have a rules problem. I look to referee C and he blubbers. I look to referee B and it's like, 'bang, bang, bang, we have this, this and this and here's the rule.' I know which official I'd follow." Crawford's comment reinforces the idea that you and I can *become* leaders, or become *better* leaders, simply by studying. Knowledge and competency are key leadership characteristics. The tall guy with the broad shoulders and a solid chin might *look* more like a leader than the one who looks rather nerdy. But if the one with the uninspiring appearance is more confident, knowledgeable, and competent, it is to him or her that people are going to look when they need leadership.

Imagine a lady named Shelley. Shelley walks into a meeting and everyone has a sense that she "has it." She exudes that special something that makes her a leader. She has nothing to prove. She is not overbearing. She just "has it." That "it" is the confidence that comes from knowing what she's doing. She obviously does her homework, and it pays off. While others have TV remotes in their hands, she is holding a leadership book, the new policy proposal, or a copy of the Scriptures in hers. Confidence cannot be faked. The confidence Shelley projects in public results from her choice to study in private.

"Be prepared in season and out of season," wrote the apostle Paul (2 Tim. 4:2). Do the hard work of preparation, and when the opportunity comes to exercise strong leadership, you will be ready. Bluffing won't cut it when someone looks at you needing a decision. You will either speak confidently because you are prepared, or you will stumble around groping for something to say and miss your opportunity for meaningful influence.

For the spiritual leader, "being prepared" involves knowledge of several things. For example, it involves a thorough understanding of the organization you lead and a grasp of the issues shaping our culture. It also involves a never-ending quest to understand the universal principles of leadership, as well as a thirst for, and knowledge of, Holy Scripture.

Nothing can substitute for intellectual and professional growth. That growth facilitates the growth of the organization and models for those around you the importance of personal development. Greater knowledge and insight must be an endless pursuit.

Reading is essential to personal growth. John Wesley was so convinced that reading was critical to ministry that he told young Methodist ministers to either read or leave vocational ministry.[20] Reading is certainly one of the most important ways you can expand your understanding and challenge your views.

Besides reading, we can take advantage of a wide range of educational opportunities. Your local college, university, or seminary probably offers a lot of helpful courses. Individualized distance learning is now offered by many highly reputable universities and seminaries.

Your education should not stop with your last seminary class. And if you are too busy to keep learning, then you are too busy. Make adjustments to your schedule. Commit to being a lifelong learner. Your intellectual health requires it.

Keep Watch over Your *Physical* Health

A few years ago I heard Ken Blanchard, a leadership guru, say, "I believe God has a lot left for me to do in this world. I don't want to cut that short by not taking care of my body." That statement from such an admirable leader continues to inspire me. I have my own calling and my own dreams. I don't want a poorly maintained body to stop me short of the goal line.

This story by Marshall Shelley is worth repeating:

> One small-town pastor in the Midwest, who counts among his congregation the widow of the former pastor, was confronted by her Sunday morning. "I tried to call you this week," she said. "Your wife told me it was your day off. I'll have you know my husband never took a day off in twenty-three years of ministry." The pastor stifled an urge to point out that her husband had also died at age forty-five.[21]

Fitness is awfully important when it comes to leadership in tough situations. Exercise makes you more alert for those quick decisions and even produces chemicals that enhance your enjoyment of life. Rest and a good diet provide the energy you need for the challenges you face. You are far more likely to make the right call if you are physically sharp.

It would be a shame to let poor health limit you. Your church desperately needs a good shepherd/leader, your family loves you, and your friends enjoy having you around. If you don't take care of yourself, many of the things God planned for you to do will go undone. The world needs you to be at your best.

According to 1 Corinthians 6:19–20, this matter is a big deal: "Do you not know that your body is a temple of the Holy Spirit, who is in you, whom you have received from God? You are not your own; you were bought at a price. Therefore honor God with your [body]." Your body is sacred space. That miraculous combination of bones, muscles, brain cells, nerve endings, connective tissue, and organ tissue that you dressed this morning—that is the temple of the Holy Spirit. Taking care of our bodies is an essential element of living as a follower of Jesus and a vital issue for spiritual leaders.

Here are some things you can do to restore and maintain your physical health.

1. Get a physical exam once a year.

So much happens in our bodies every day, and we remain completely unaware of most of it. We need bodily experts to check us out. An annual physical exam by a licensed medical professional will help ensure our health, including catching at an early stage what might be undermining our bodies in ways we might never dream until it could be too late.

2. Exercise regularly.

I fear that too many vocational ministers are getting too little exercise. Oh, some of us are busy jumping through hoops, beating the bushes, and running in circles. But that's not the kind of exercise I'm talking about. Exercise, real physical exercise, builds our heart, strengthens our bones and muscles, expands our lungs, and helps us maintain our weight or lose some of the excess weight. Exercise also releases within the body endorphins—chemicals that contribute to our mental health, "abundant life chemicals." Every time you pump that iron or take a step on the treadmill or pedal that bike, your body produces a tiny amount of chemicals that God designed to make us more energetic and more positive about life.

I'm not talking about exercise for the purpose of having a body like a Greek god or goddess. I'm talking about proper care of the bodies with which God has blessed us. If we are going to be our best in service to Him and others, we need to be as healthy as we can be.

Moreover, the self-discipline of exercise strengthens our characters as well as our bodies. Some of us ministers would be less shabby, less flabby, and even less crabby if we'd get off our gluteus maximuses!

3. Go to bed.

A lot of research demonstrates the danger of too many hours awake. Getting enough sleep actually makes us more efficient and productive. If we are borrowing from our sleep in order to do something else, like church work, we are getting a negative return on our investment.

4. Have fun.

Look for hobbies and other kinds of diversions that break your routine. Football officiating is a wonderful diversion for me. Several times a week during the fall I grab my flag, whistle, and striped shirt, and go have some fun.

In 2012 I took up golf and hiking. The new hobbies have been great for my emotional health. I am always looking forward to the next day I will be in the woods or on the golf course, and my quality of life is significantly better.

Hiking, golfing, and getting yelled at by football fans might not be on your list of enjoyable diversions. So find diversions that work for you.

5. Eat right.

When I say "eat right," I'm not talking about completely avoiding everything that tastes good. After all, the Bible talks about feasts. I'm talking about balance—moderation, if you will. I'm talking about remembering that "food pyramid" I learned as a kid (or whatever they had when *you* were a kid) and the need to eat food from all the food groups. I'm talking about pushing back from the table at the right time almost all the time. Then, from time to time, we can say, "Aunt Ethyl, that chocolate pie is so good I'm going to have one more half a piece."

I'm not talking about fad diets or unhealthy diets. I'm talking about good sense and eating right. I'm talking about limiting the fats, salt, and sugar. I like Bill Hybels's warning. He encouraged us to eat "lots of delicious high fiber foods—fruits and vegetables, whole grain breads and cereals, nuts, figs, dates," and so on. And he responded to the inevitable protests: "'But wait,' you say, 'That's what those flakes in California eat.' That's right. And I visit there a lot and see sixty-year-old men roller skating along the Pacific Coast and winking at girls on the beach. Meanwhile, forty-five-year-old Midwesterners are making their first appointment at the Mayo Clinic. Think about it."[22]

It would be hypocritical of me to suggest that you should never eat between meals or that you should eat *only* really healthy foods. My wife Keri would laugh out loud if I were to even imply that I never snack and eat only healthy stuff. But I can, in good conscience, suggest that we eat sensibly and in moderation.

6. Practice creative Sabbaths.

I've been saving this one for last.

The commandment about keeping the Sabbath holy is perhaps the toughest commandment to apply to our lives today. This isn't

Sinai, 1500 B.C. It isn't Mayberry, 1950, either. We've got more fish to fry, more irons in the fire, and more plates to keep spinning than they did back then. We're up to our eyeballs in alligators. We're swimming with the sharks. So how do we practice a Sabbath in a frenzied, nonstop culture like ours?

We get creative. Because of today's lifestyles, I suggest we take "creative Sabbaths." I say "creative Sabbaths" because, with a minister's schedule, expecting the opportunity to do absolutely nothing one day per week might be impractical for you.

I believe Jesus himself practiced "creative Sabbaths." He wasn't so strict about a particular day, but he understood the value of the Sabbath principle. He carved out rest breaks in the middle of his week, sometimes realizing that he was becoming used up. As I heard somewhere, he often *came apart* so that he wouldn't *come apart*.

So follow Jesus' example and take mini-Sabbaths. Take a long walk. Take a power nap. Turn your phone off for a while. Take a week. Take a day. Take the advice from the commercial that says, "Support the local babysitting industry, and go out to eat." The basic point is that you need down time. You need sacred space. You need a day, or a couple of half days, or three one-third days, when you are Sabbathing. You need Sabbath time. *When* you take it is not something to get too hung up over.

I think worrying about the particulars of how we are to celebrate, and what we can and cannot do, robs the Sabbath of its celebratory mood. If you were to give Keri and me a gift certificate for a meal at a great restaurant, for example, then you wouldn't be hung up on which night Keri and I went. Or what we wore. Or whether we ordered steak or chicken. The only way to misuse that gift would be not to use it.

If we don't take advantage of the gift of Sabbath-rest, we will suffer the consequences—physical, emotional, and spiritual ones. We will suffer in terms of our relationships and joy.

One of my seminary friends seemed to have limitless energy. He was a husband, a full-time student, and a father of three boys. He served a church as part-time pastor. And he worked at least twenty hours a week at a downtown bank. I remember clearly his saying to me one day, "I believe God has given me an unusual ability to sleep only a few hours and still accomplish many tasks."

Then one Saturday night he ended up in a Louisville emergency room diagnosed with exhaustion.

We need our rest. Not just sleep. Rest. Downtime. Relaxed time. Chill time. Laidback time. Hakuna Matata time. If you aren't willing to rest, you might have a faith problem. If you aren't willing to rest, you might be a megalomaniac. If you aren't willing to rest, you might be confusing significance with productivity.

I can't say enough about the importance of physical self-care. Our physical condition has a direct impact on our mental condition. It fascinated me to learn that chess masters work hard at being in top physical shape. Chess players! Brainiacs! Those guys who play perhaps the most sedentary game imaginable! Yet they know that their mental acumen, their ability to maintain concentration, is dependent on a healthy body. So if you want to have a sharp mind as well as a strong spirit, get your body in shape. And that includes getting needed rest, needed Sabbaths.

Keep Watch over the *Well-Being of Your Family*

Inevitable risk to your family comes with a call to vocational ministry. Countless are the spouses and children of ministers who have been hurt and discouraged because of criticisms of ministers they love. That comes with the territory. There is a limit, however, to the pain to which the minister should subject his or her loved ones. While the sons and daughters of ministers can learn great lessons about poise and divine strength in the midst of an attack, those lessons might come at too great a cost.

While writing this, my wife and I visited our youngest son, Grant, where he is working as a graduate assistant at a large university. I had a leisurely conversation with one of Grant's co-workers, a man of about fifty. "Grant tells me you're a pastor," he said. "My daddy was a pastor, too…and it drove me from the church. It wasn't how hurt my daddy was; it was how much they hurt my mom."

Charles Chandler, Executive Director of *Ministering to Ministers Foundation,* noted that "during church conflict and forced terminations, ministers' spouses usually experience more pain, have more anger, and recover from the trauma more slowly than the minister."[23]

So when should we ministers stay and when should we say, "Enough is enough"? I suggest that some churches are not worth the pain of your family. Neither church bullies nor the folks who let bullies have their way deserve for you to sacrifice your spouse and/or children. Of course, almost any leadership role—from politics to coaching little league to the neighborhood association—will result in your family worrying about how people are treating you. You will have to weigh the depth of your loved ones' suffering against the mission and potential of your church and then make a decision you can sleep with.

Keep Watch over Your *Thoughts and Behavior*

"Keeping watch over ourselves" means monitoring and nurturing the many aspects of our health. It also means controlling ourselves. Nothing can substitute for self-control—the decision to live a holy life. President Harry Truman said, "In reading the lives of great men, I found that the first victory they won was over themselves… [S]elf-discipline with all of them came first."[24]

The New Testament speaks often of the need for self-control. If you read through the little book of Titus, in chapter 2 alone you will find words translated as "self-controlled" five times. In verses 11–12, for example, the writer says, "[T]he grace of God…teaches us to say 'No' to ungodliness and worldly passions, and to live self-controlled…lives."

The Greek words translated "self-control" in our English versions of Scripture—*egkrateia* and *sophronismos*—teach us the importance of "getting a grip," taking hold of situations, feelings, areas of our lives that are out of control. To encapsulate the full meaning of the Greek words, we would need to use several English words: *self-discipline, self-control, good sense, moderation, prudence, sober-mindedness, sound mind,* and "*temperance*" (as it is translated in the *King James* version). Self-control for a leader often means taking a deep breath and dialing it down when on the inside we are feeling panic, fear, or anger.

When we think of self-control, most of us think *negatively,* considering what *not* to do, what to avoid. But here are two positive ways in which I have learned to think of self-control: (1) delayed gratification, and (2) a deep, burning "yes" that enables us to say "no." Of course, delayed gratification is saying "no" to short-term pleasure, even experiencing short-term pain. But it is more than a no; it is also saying yes to the long-term benefits that are possible as a result of the waiting. As for the second idea, it comes out clearly in the work of Steven Covey. He teaches that self-control at its best grows out of what he calls a "passion of vision"—a passionate commitment to values that releases within us an energy and motivation to do that which is in harmony with those values. This "passion of vision" is a passion for that which is really important; it empowers us to say "no" to things that are unimportant.[25] Driven by our values and principles, all else pales in comparison to that passion of vision. So we are empowered to say yes to what matters and no to what doesn't.

Self-control comes into play when you and I are under pressure—perhaps in a meeting that is not going well, or in a conversation in which we are being unfairly attacked. First Timothy 3:1–7 speaks of the importance of the role of "overseer" and includes in the list of qualifications these words: "temperate, self-controlled,… not violent but gentle, not quarrelsome." In The Message, those ideas are expressed like this: "cool and collected, accessible,… not pushy but gentle, not thin-skinned." In short, we must be poised—carefully avoiding the outbursts that might temporarily feel so good—for the sake of the greater vision.

But there's still more to self-control. There is another qualifier in that 1 Timothy 3 passage. In *The Message* it says "committed to his wife." Self-control includes deciding now that we will be faithful to our spouses physically and emotionally.

I had returned from more than four years in Africa and was having lunch with a long-time minister friend who was catching me up on what I'd missed while overseas. Sadly, many of his updates were about ministerial sex scandals on the local and national level. I don't think I'll ever forget the way my friend summed up the situation: "My new definition of ministerial hero is someone who can keep his pants zipped up."

Keeping one's self spiritually healthy, and making sure one's marriage is strong are essential. But they aren't enough. We simply cannot allow ourselves to be in tempting situations. That means, in my opinion, being rather prudish about some things. As a pastor I didn't go to lunch with ladies, for example. I talk about Keri in my sermons, so that everyone knows how much I love her. I don't converse about intimate emotional issues with female friends. And as a pastor I'd heard enough stories of affairs that began in counseling sessions that my radar was always on.

Keri and I acknowledged to each other years ago that we are human and thus vulnerable. Therefore we entered into a covenant that includes those preventative practices that I mentioned in the previous paragraph. People in many professions cannot afford the kind of safeguards, perhaps, that I have put in place. But in our ministerial profession, I feel we cannot afford *not* to practice those safeguards.

This is a big deal, so may I be candid? *Keep your pants on.*

When my brother-in-law, Keith, was a teenager, church was not his favorite activity. One Sunday morning he was sitting in the balcony with a fellow bored teen during the 11:00 a.m. worship service. One of them had brought a box of BBs. The balcony floor is hardwood and has tiers. The two mischievous boys were sitting on the upper level, on the back row against the wall. In the middle of the pastor's proclamation, one of them dropped the box of BBs. Those little, loud balls of steel rolled and crashed and rolled and crashed to the delight of some, the anger of Keith's mother who was watching from the choir loft, the discombobulation of the preacher, and the near death of the boys when they got home. Here's my point. Those two boys probably were not the only ones bored that morning. They weren't the only ones "out of line." They just had high profiles. If they had been downstairs, the BBs would have fallen on the carpet and only a few congregants might have looked at them in scorn. But given where they were sitting in the church and the wooden floor beneath them, *everybody* knew it when they messed up!

Likewise, when a minister fails morally, the impact is wider than it is for most people. You have the kind of profile that makes the BB's you drop more disruptive than those dropped by others. That principle is found in Luke 12:3, "What you have said in the dark will be heard in the daylight, and what you have whispered in the ear in the inner rooms will be proclaimed from the roofs." Calvin Miller used that verse to warn young pastors about the potential impact of sexual sins: "I enjoin you: Be aware of those discoveries that set you naked on a rooftop and shout to all the world, 'Here was a foolish man who was never wise enough to fear.'"[26]

We never will rise above our vulnerability, but we can practice self-control and thereby keep our vulnerability in check.

What Now?

"Keep watch over yourselves," Paul advised (Acts 20:28). No doubt he knew what the battle-scarred and decorated veteran of the pastorate, Bill Self, knew when he wrote:

> So much of the lore of ministry has to do with sacrifice, martyrdom, and self-denial. The heroes of the faith are thrown into the lions' den, crucified upside down, imprisoned for long stretches of time, but not much is said about taking care of yourself so that you can serve longer and better, keeping your mind fresh so that you can think straighter, or making sure that your body is well-serviced and maintained so that it will not wear out before its time. A tired and beat-up pastor will not grow spiritually or professionally.[27]

The joys and chores, ups and downs, victories and pitfalls of the pastorate are basically what they were two thousand years ago. To accomplish the work, we need to take care of ourselves, not just our congregations. So take some time. Count the cost. Be honest with yourself. What do you need to change? What do you need to give up? What do you need to add? What do you need to do to keep watch over yourself? You, your family, your friends, and your congregation need you to take good care of yourself.

4

All the Flock

"...and all the flock..."

*"My wife, who is an attorney, can 'fire' a client who is
too difficult to work with. If a doctor's care is continually
criticized by a patient, that doctor can refuse to offer
further treatment and refer the patient to another doctor.
A restaurant manager can refuse service to a recalcitrant
customer. But pastors are expected to care for those they did
not choose and perhaps would never have chosen under any
other circumstances. The church, like the family, is a place
where we try to learn to live with those we are stuck with...
As a pastor, I am expected to care about people I may not
particularly care for."*

—Pastor Martin B. Copenhavor, in
This Odd and Wondrous Calling.[1]

Picking and choosing which sheep to keep watch over is not an
option for the Christian minister. God gives us a people to serve,
a flock to protect, a congregation to love. The whole bunch—not
just some of them.

No one ever said we'd enjoy everyone equally. "Keeping watch
over all the flock" has nothing to do with personal preferences,
common interests, and generational compatibility. I, for example,
have always preferred people who like the things I like and think
I'm the best pastor they've ever known. Care for the entire flock,
however, demands more than similarities and mutual admiration.
Sometimes it takes real discipline. *Love,* remember, is also a verb.

We might as well admit it; some of the sheep don't like *us*, the *shepherds*. I don't mean they merely prefer other ministers' styles; I mean they *don't like us*. Still, we are called to shepherd them, too. We are called to speak to people who will fold their arms and won't look us in the eye while we're preaching or teaching. We are called to be kind to people who would not be on our side if a vote-of-confidence were held tomorrow. We are called to sit through meetings with people who know (and will never forget the fact that) the last decision we made was disastrous. We are called to roll out our perception of God's vision to people who saw us bungle the last question we were asked publicly about the church budget. We are called to comfort people who have been mean to us, to marry people whose parents wanted another minister, and to applaud the good work of people whose attitudes we don't like. We are called to visit emergency rooms and funeral parlors, to sit at the table in the Fellowship Hall and church picnic, and to worship and go on mission trips with people about whom we've thought un-ministerial thoughts.

Furthermore, we are called to speak of holy and pure things to people who know we are guilty of unholy thoughts and impure motives. We are called to speak of biblical truths that many of our listeners have mastered better than we have. We are called to lead people who could do certain aspects of our job better than we can.

In short, we are called to keep watch over *all* the flock. No exceptions.

Of course, each congregation is made up of various groups and personalities. Ministering to each of them has its own rewards and challenges.

The Old and the Young

Winn Collier, a young church planter, once told me, "The day of the single generation church is gone." Another young church planter (whose name I cannot remember) told me, "A lot of people come in through our doors but then eventually move on to a congregation that also has *older folks*," gesturing toward me. The research I see confirms their observations. Robert Webber wrote: "The younger evangelicals desire to be around their parents and grandparents, and their dislike of being separated into their own group runs counter to the advice given by the church-growth movements that the way to grow a church is to target generations.

Today's younger people seek out intergenerational communities where they mix and form relationships with all ages."[2]

All that being said, successfully orchestrating the efforts of diverse generations takes great skill, for each group has its weaknesses as well as its strengths. I love Peter Scazzero's quote: "The church is full of younger sons running away every time God or someone else does not meet their expectations. It is also full of older brothers who are angry and grumpy."[3]

I have not always done a good job balancing the challenges of each group. For example, I led the church I most recently served to embrace a vision we called "A Mejor Mañana" (A Better Tomorrow). The core of that vision was to engage young adults, whom we identified as ages 18 to 39. When I saw Psalm 71:18, I sensed that God had a word for me: "Even when I am old and gray, / do not forsake me, O God, / till I declare your power to the next generation, / your mighty acts to all who are to come."

I believe one of my callings is to be a bridge from my generation to the next. So a "Mejor Mañana" is part of my pastoral identity. Therefore, when I cast this vision to my church, I painted a picture of our church's future with lots of young adults coming. What I unintentionally failed to communicate in this picture of an ideal future is that older adults would be coming, too. I failed to adequately regard, affirm, and champion the causes dear to our older adults. I let wonderful people feel like they didn't matter to me because of my perceived myopic focus on the future. Frankly, I was disappointed because the response felt rather self-interested. Yet I had to admit that I had not been adequately inclusive in my vision-casting. I was blessed to have an older man take me to lunch and speak straight to me. "Some folks my age feel like they aren't being heard," he told me. So I hosted a series of small gatherings during which I listened to people easily old enough to be my parents. I learned a lot in those conversations, and I hope I communicated my true desire to be the pastor of all generations.

It's simply not an option. For one thing, ministering to everyone is our calling; it's the right thing. Besides that, multi-generational churches are the best churches. Multi-generational churches enjoy the energy, drive, and new ideas of young members as well as the stability, wisdom, and history of older members. Members in the middle have leadership potential, earning power, and teenaged children to build the youth program. The Church needs them all.

The Sweet and the Sour

I know what it's like to preach to people who won't look me in the eye—people who sit looking at the floor the entire time I'm speaking as if looking at me might somehow legitimize me. I know what it's like to have my integrity—not merely my decisions, but my integrity—questioned in front of a room full of people. I've done those difficult things I mentioned earlier, such as sitting in emergency rooms with people who don't like me and marrying people whose parents would have preferred another minister. I've been at this kind of work a long time, so I know what it's like to minister to sour people.

I also know what it's like to minister to people who are much sweeter than I deserve. I know what it's like to be wrong, and for people to know I am wrong. I know what it's like for people to pay me compliments I don't merit, to give me more credit than is warranted, to assume my motives are more pure than they are.

Most of the people, honestly, are in the "sweet" category. Overwhelmingly so. Wonderfully so. Honestly, I was blessed with healthy congregations. The "sweet" ones far outnumbered the "sour" ones. It's just that the ones I often thought most about were in the "sour" category.[4] Maurice Graham, founder of Shepherd's Staff, put it this way:

> In my initial research in 2000–2001, talking to 200 pastors and 200 lay leaders…one of my findings was…80% of people…are actively involved with passive, peace-loving, non-aggressive personalities. 20% of the congregation has more assertive to aggressive personalities. Within that 20% there is a 5% of the total that are super aggressive. They are the ones that are demanding and confronting and create most of the ill will in the congregation.[5]

Even sour folks have their place in the family. I love the story about the man named Gurdjieff, the leader of a spiritual community in Russia and then Paris. He was a rather odd sort of fellow. However, he did have at least one important insight into human character. Gurdjieff had a community, a commune-like group of folks who lived in community with him and his other students. One of the members of that community was a crotchety guy no one liked. Finally, the old crab got so tired of being on the outs with everybody else that he left the community altogether.

Everyone was relieved that the pain-in-the-neck had gone. Everyone except Gurdjieff. Gurdjieff followed the malcontent to Paris and tried to convince him to return to the community. He refused, so Gurdjieff offered to pay the guy's expenses if he'd only come back. All the other students were paying to live in Gurdjieff's community, but Gurdjieff was going to actually pay this guy to live there!

Well, when the cranky old man agreed to return to the community, the others there were outraged, particularly when they found out he was being paid to be there. Gurdjieff explained the method in his madness: "You came to me so that I could help you work on your maturity, the development of your character. You need this man among you so that you will learn patience and compassion."[6]

There are limits to the divisive behavior a community should tolerate. However, spiritual maturity comes from the discipline of choosing to love people whom we find difficult to love. And all of us, at times, are difficult for at least *somebody* to love.

Oh, by the way, the people you become the most angry with might not be the sour ones; they might be the sweet ones who privately tell you how much they love you and then stand by and say nothing while the unfiltered super-aggressives hurt you and the church. No matter. You have to keep watch over them, too.

The Supporters and Opposers of Your Vision

No matter how carefully you plan and pray, some people will not be on board with the vision you cast. Some won't "get it." Others will get it but they will simply disagree that it is a valid vision for this moment in the church's history. Some, of course, will oppose anything that might suggest change. Many will grant lukewarm approval to your proposals while a great number will jump up on top of the wave with you and ride it into the future. You'll have to keep watch over them all. It will be rather easy to serve those who agree with you. A real test of your heart and your head will be how you deal with those who don't. A good leader will not dismiss those who don't whole-heartedly embrace his or her dream. And a good leader will not demonize the detractors.

Distinguishing troublemakers from the loyal opposition can be difficult. The fact that people vote "no" in a business meeting does not make them bad persons. It's true that some folks are rabble-rousers and mischief-makers. But we must not assume that all who disagree with our decisions are Tobiahs and Sanballets—the two antagonists who pooh-poohed Nehemiah's plan for rebuilding Jerusalem's walls, taunted the Jews and did everything they could to derail the project.

Furthermore, negative attitudes and comments can be beneficial to the organization. The doubter keeps the dreamer in check.

Now let's be clear: the mission of the church cannot afford for you to spend *too much* time among people who don't support it. You cannot ignore them, of course, for their opposition can help shape the direction of the church by helping you and others refine the vision. They cannot, however, be allowed to determine either your schedule or the church's mission.

The Healthy and the Unhealthy

Emotionally unhealthy people can be rather sadistic.

I was walking down the hall of a Kentucky nursing home one day when an elderly lady called me over. "Aren't you going to speak to me?!" she snapped. I never had seen the lady, but in her mind I was someone who should have been attentive to her. It was clear that the poor lady was not completely "with it," yet I decided to play along. I walked over and told her how sorry I was that I didn't acknowledge her. My apology did not assuage her displeasure.

She asked, curtly, "What's that on your shirt, an ink spot?"

"No ma'am," I said, "that's a horse." (I was wearing a Polo shirt that I'd probably bought at the outlet store.) Trying to be cute, I added, "This is my cowboy shirt!"

"Well, that's a good shirt for you!" she said with a glower and grimace. "You old jackass!"

If someone else had said that, I would have been offended, but not so with this lady. This was not personal. She didn't even know me. Her mind was playing tricks on her, and somehow I must have represented someone or something that made her angry. I understood that she was not healthy. I was easily able to dismiss her attack.

Many of the attacks directed at you will be much like that. While a few of them may come from people with dementia, some of the particularly vicious and malicious attacks will instead come from people who are intelligent yet suffer from an underlying unhealthiness. To them, you may represent something or someone who makes them angry.

James 4:1 reminds us that battles between us are usually the result of battles within us. It's a little easier to remain poised when we remember that so many of the people in our congregations are battling within—hurting silently and deeply. That does not excuse malicious behavior, but it does make it more understandable.

Careful now: Don't write off everyone who criticizes you as crazy. Simply remember that many folks are not as mean as they are unhealthy. Consider that fact when you are trying to figure out how to respond to an attack and how to keep watch over them as a shepherd who cares.

Those Who Like the New Temple and Those Who Don't

In Ezra 3:10–13 I found a fascinating story. Solomon's Temple—an architectural wonder and the depository of so many good memories—was the heart and soul, the centerpiece, of the ancient Hebrews. This grand structure was destroyed, along with most of Jerusalem, by the Babylonian army in 587 B.C. Fifty years later, as people began to return to Jerusalem, Zerubbabel led in the construction of a new temple. When the foundation of the new temple—called Zerubbabel's Temple—was laid, those who had not known the former temple shouted for joy. They cheered for Zerubbabel, thrilled to have a place to call their own as their predecessors had. But those who had worshiped in *Solomon's* Temple wept so loudly one could not distinguish the cheering from the crying. Why? Because the new temple was not the old. The new temple was not as impressive, not as ornate as the old one. For some people, the new temple didn't seem as sacred as the former had been. They saw the new temple as a poor imitation of the real thing.

We can understand the feelings of both groups. We can understand why it was painful to see something as meaningful as Solomon's Temple replaced. We can also understand why those who had not known the Temple of Solomon were delighted that they were going to have a place where they, too, could sense the presence of God—where God would meet them and accept their offerings.

Vocational ministers are servant leaders to both groups—fans of the old temple and fans of the new. We simply need to understand the dynamics of both groups in order to minister to them.

You might have to be intentional about appreciating those who like the "old temple"—the way the church used to look and feel, the way their favorite pastor used to preach, the way decisions used to involve everyone, the week-long revivals, and other cherished traditions to which people would like to cling. It's important that we recognize what those who built the church are feeling as their church undergoes inevitable change. We must do our best to keep people from feeling marginalized and ignored.

Older people get stereotyped as stubbornly resistant to anything new, and the stereotype is not without its supporting evidence. But I love the advice that Will Willimon gave to a young pastor who was decrying the so-called stuck-in-the-ruts old folks in his congregation. Willimon noted that some of life's biggest changes come after age sixty-five—changes such as declining health, loss of independence, unemployment, and the loss of a spouse. So Willimon advised the young pastor:

> It's not fair to say that these older people are refusing to change. They are about to drown in some of the most dramatic changes life offers. When you've buried the man you have lived with for forty years, or you are forced out of your life work, about the last thing you want is to come to church and have some upstart young preacher say, "Let's do something new and innovative today." They're sinking in a flood of innovation.[7]

Understand too that a skeptical attitude toward change is not limited to older people. A friend who is much younger than I am posted this on her Facebook page: "'Change' is not the same thing as 'improvement.' Accusing someone of having 'a fear of change' when they disagree w/you and offer an alternative to your 'change' that you do not like, instead of debating the issues head-on, will not earn you respect or 'converts' to your position." My friend was talking about a school system, not a church. But her words are applicable in your congregation. Make sure people like her are heard, no matter what their age.

Naturally, you will need to listen as well to those who thrive on change. Do not let their positive voices get drowned out by the loud and often strident voices of naysayers. For most of us, of course, it is easier to hear the voice of someone encouraging progress than that of someone telling us to take our progress and go somewhere else. The point is that you are the servant leader of both groups. Just keep that in mind and respond to them accordingly.

The Big Wheels and the Little Wheels

I want to remind you of this section in the book of James:

My brothers and sisters, believers in our glorious Lord Jesus Christ must not show favoritism. Suppose a man comes into your meeting wearing a gold ring and fine clothes, and a poor man in filthy old clothes also comes in. If you show special attention to the man wearing fine clothes and say, "Here's a good seat for you," but say to the poor man, "You stand there" or "Sit on the floor by my feet," have you not discriminated among yourselves and become judges with evil thoughts? (Jas. 2:1-4)

One of the sweetest ladies I know once confessed something to me that was really embarrassing to her. She told me, "Travis, I've held something for a long time and I just have to get it off my chest." Then she told the story.

She had worshiped in the 9:30 morning worship service at our church and then headed to the parking lot. She was standing, waiting for a friend, when she noticed an old pickup truck pulling into the parking lot. She admitted that she wondered what someone in a rather unsightly truck might be doing at her church. As she stood there she noticed that the pickup was driving toward her. She was somewhat uncomfortable when the driver of the pickup pulled up next to her, and she admitted she looked down to avoid eye contact. Then she heard the truck's window rolling down and she thought, *Whoever this is wants to talk to me!*

Then she slowly looked up—and recognized the driver of that old pickup truck that looked so out of place. It was I, the senior pastor of her church.

We'd had a guest speaker that morning and I'd been visiting another of our campuses. I had driven back for the 11:00 service in my everyday vehicle, an old pickup truck, and noticed this lady standing out there alone. She was looking down, and I wanted to make sure she was alright!

This sweet lady (so sweet that she gave me permission to tell that story), a faithful and wonderful Christian, admitted that she was significantly less excited about an old pickup truck pulling into the church parking lot than she would have been in seeing a newer and more fashionable vehicle. And, as nice as she is, if *she* had those feelings, *any* of us could have those feelings.

In fact, I am convinced this is a real problem in most of our churches: the very favoritism—a shallow, arrogant, elitist favoritism—against which Scripture so poignantly warns in the book of James.

This is such a simple thing, but it is nevertheless profound: We must not practice favoritism at churches. And it's not just about welcoming outsiders from all rungs of the socio-economic ladder. It's about treating all the family members with equal respect, no matter—let's just be candid—no matter their giving potential.

Of course everyone does not carry the same weight in church-wide decisions. The person who is spiritually mature and has invested lots in the church over the years is understandably and justifiably going to speak with more authority than will some others. However, the spiritually mature person with less potential to contribute financially, yet who has given faithfully from what he or she has, absolutely must have the same respect granted as does the one with greater giving capacity. Where that is not true, we have an integrity problem.

If people are buying influence in our congregations, shame on us. If we are allowing anyone to threaten leaders with the fear that he or she will withhold money if a decision doesn't go his or her way, shame on them *and* us. If there is anywhere that social hierarchy doesn't mean anything, it should be the family of God. It's the principle of the widow's mite, and Jesus had something to say about that.

The N's and the S's

When I was still pastoring a church, our church staff took the *Myers-Briggs Personality Indicator* as an attempt to better understand each other's operational styles. One of the most important revelations I had was not about interactions among the staff, but about interaction between the ministerial staff and the congregation. Most of us on the staff tested out as N's (Intuitors). We N's make certain decisions because our intuition tells us that's the right thing to do. When we come to decisions, we've often been down similar roads before, so deciding is largely a matter of "feel." S's (Sensors), on the other hand, like to make decisions based on an abundance of gathered data. An S would say, "Know the facts, and analyze the facts, and then make a well-informed decision."

Our staff had a whole bunch of N's. My educated guess, my "holy hunch," was that our congregation had a whole bunch of S's. That hunch led me to an important insight. Sometimes I (and others) had brought decisions to church meetings based on our informed intuition. We Intuitors had a deep sense of rightness and expected others to embrace our ideas with the same kind of enthusiasm we had. But the S's (Sensors) in our church understandably wanted plenty of data, analysis, and demonstrable facts. Moreover, somewhere along the way there very well may have been some 'N-style' leaders who merely followed their hunches and thus led the church off a cliff.

So, sometimes we N's felt unsupported, misunderstood, and distrusted by the S's. And sometimes the S's must have thought the N's were being irresponsible. N's and S's seemed at odds; in reality, they each simply had different-yet-valid approaches to problems.

As ministers, we need to understand that both intuition and analysis have their places. What is important is that we realize that among us there are two basic (and very different) decision-making styles, and we need to accommodate each one. My insight led me to make a public apology to the S's in our congregation for my part in bringing to them decisions I and others had intuited and just expected everyone to embrace. I wish I had known about the impact on our church of this Intuitor/Sensor thing long ago. Some of our early decisions might have gone a bit smoother.

The Paid Staff and the Volunteers

How one supervises a paid worker and how one supervises a volunteer are two different things. Oh, I know that volunteers deserve both adequate training and high expectations. And volunteers can be fired. I also know that true leadership is based on influence and inspiration, not paychecks. But there still is a real difference in the way that we direct those who get paid for us to lead them and those who don't.

Among other reasons, those who volunteer are motivated by the satisfaction that comes from making a significant contribution to a significant cause. Of course, that's true of paid people, too, but the addition of that paycheck is no small motivation—a motivation that volunteers lack.

You will have to develop your situational leadership skills in order to shift from staff leadership to volunteer leadership and back. Don't indulge the volunteers such that your staff members resent how differently you act among the staff. Make sure the paid staff ministers feel as valued as do the volunteers. And remember that both volunteers and staff honor you by being part of your team.

Even the Saboteurs

"Saboteurs" is the word that Steve Bagi gives to the people who intentionally or unintentionally jeopardize both the church's health and yours. Bagi writes:

Most saboteurs in their hearts believe that they are serving Jesus, defending the pillars of faith and decency and yet do not realize the cloud of stress that follows them daily. They have always been in churches; just ask Paul when you see him. They are not a new phenomenon but how they are handled may be. In our political niceness they are often not put into place.

...Often nothing is said to or done with the saboteur. No one speaks up because it's not the nice thing to do. Leaders sometimes carry not only the pain caused by saboteurs but also the disappointment of the inaction of their church family to stand with them in the fight.

...In our attempt to be fair and democratic we have sometimes allowed people to take the floor who shouldn't have even been allowed into the meeting. There is cost to confrontation, but sadly there is a greater cost to chickening out...[8]

Sometimes the pastoral thing to do is to find a kind but firm way to say, "You're out of line." Negative people must not be allowed to set the agenda for the organization.

When dealing with difficult people, the following truths have been helpful to me:

1. Remember: Your church has a sinner for its pastor.

It is important to stand firmly against the manipulation and mutiny of difficult people. It is equally important that we not always assume the difficult person is someone else. In the words of Eugene Peterson, "Every congregation is a congregation of sinners. As if that weren't bad enough, they all have sinners for pastors."[9]

2. Labeling people is dangerous.

The Bible does label. Titus 3:10, for example, says, "Warn a divisive person once, and then warn them a second time. After that, have nothing to do with them." The Bible says, "a divisive person." Scripture labels him or her, and says, "Don't let that person hurt the church. He or she is a divisive person."

But you and I cannot claim the same level of inspiration in our everyday thinking that the apostle Paul could claim in writing Scripture. So we need to tread lightly here.

In my library, I have two very different books on this subject. One is Paul Meier's book *Don't Let Jerks Get the Best of You*; the other is Arthur Boer's book *Never Call Them Jerks*! I deeply appreciate Meier's warning not to let unhealthy people rob us of our joy. However, Boer makes a great point—if we label people, we make it easy on ourselves to dismiss them. Once I label someone a knucklehead or knothead, blockhead, or bonehead, I've dehumanized him or her. I know it's true because I've done it. Instead of seeing them as flesh-and-blood individuals, as moms and dads, as people with hurts, fears, dreams, and goals, they become objects—objects that don't deserve our energy, our understanding, or our love. Anne Jackson wrote: "Some of the greatest leaders I know have been severely hurt in ministry. I interviewed several…and I discovered this consistent insight: the leaders who were the healthiest were the ones who never disrespected the people who hurt them."[10]

Before you assume I am suggesting an overly passive approach to dealing with malicious people, please read on. You will see that, when people have established a destructive, abusive, divisive track record, it would be naïve and irresponsible to ignore that. My point here is simply that when we are too quick to attach a moniker to someone, we cut off the potential for redemptive relationship.

When we call someone a "jerk" (or similar epithet), that is often a sign of relational laziness. Moreover, it's really easy to disregard unpleasant people as unworthy of my inconvenience.

If someone has forfeited the right to your energy by repeated misbehavior, so be it; just don't go there too quickly.

3. Problems almost never "work themselves out." But sometimes they do.

Hoping sticky situations will blow over, kicking the proverbial can down the road, is often the cowardly way of dealing with things. But sometimes letting things play out is wise. Sometimes… *sometimes*…letting things work themselves out actually works. One of the roles of leadership is to do our best to determine which situations might actually resolve themselves and which ones will require our intervention.

4. Becoming the object of conflict is not something we should do casually.

Those of us who will be held responsible for decisions should think carefully before saying or doing something that will make us the object of conflict. When we are under attack, it's not good for us or for the church. If we, as leaders, gamble our leadership on too many issues, the odds are going to catch up with us. Skillful leaders do not enter every skirmish.

5. Letting the players handle things, when possible, is good leadership.

At every coin toss in the middle of a high school football field at the start of a game, I as the referee say to the captains on each team, "We officials don't want to be the rule police and we don't want to flag people, especially for unsportsmanlike conduct. So I want you guys to handle that for us, okay? Help us control your players."

Sometimes good leadership means encouraging and supporting level heads behind the scenes and not jumping into every fray. Please don't hear me saying that vocational ministers can pass the buck or hide behind laypersons. I'm simply suggesting that there are times when letting the laypersons in your church work things out is the prudent option. You don't have to be the arbitrator at every contest. Letting wise people work things out, and even letting unwise people feel the heat from their peers (if their peers are willing to speak out), may be the better part of wisdom.

6. Some church folks have great attendance records but are emotionally immature.

In the list of the fruit of the Spirit, regular attendance at church functions is not included. And emotional maturity is not always in direct proportion to the number of times someone has sat through small group sessions or Sunday school classes. So don't assume that those who are always present are those who need to drive the discussion.

7. Playing the role of victim is just not helpful.

At times I've moaned to friends about how tough my ministry was. That, however, never got me anywhere.

You are not the victim of the deacons or the elders or the Women's Circle or anybody else. They might have treated you badly, but that doesn't make you a victim. Victims have little recourse other than to yell for help. That is not you.

Besides, with the role of victim come several disadvantages: (1) our "victimizers" get in our heads; (2) we miss the opportunities to grow and change that owning our own problems brings; and (3) we aren't much fun for healthy people to be around.

8. Saboteurs do have to be confronted.

Sometimes leadership requires painful confrontation. Whenever we confront, we must do it carefully, with mature, Christlike attitudes, and only after honest self-examination. But mature leaders sometimes have to say, "That's enough. No more." Often that responsibility falls to the pastor or the minister whose ministry area is being impacted by the bad behavior.

Now, let's be careful here. I'm not talking about ministers being eager to castigate those who won't go along with their initiatives. But when the health and mission of the church are in jeopardy, the overseer's responsibility is to step in.

Our Pastor Emeritus, Bob Cochran, told me a story that haunts me. A man shot himself in the head on the grounds of one of Bob's former churches. When Bob arrived on the scene, he noted a leaf covered with the blood of the young, deceased man. Bob took the leaf home with him. That young man's death was particularly painful for Bob because the young man recently had been a guest in their worship, so he was a "prospect" for their church. The congregation had had an opportunity to make a difference in his life. Who knows? Perhaps they could have been part of a new life trajectory for this troubled young man. Yet the people of the church were embroiled in some sort of conflict—too preoccupied by their quarrels to think much about "prospects."

I've held that leaf—the leaf that bears the blood stains of the young man. Bob had it framed under glass and kept it as a reminder of what happens when churches get diverted by discord. Of course, there is no guarantee that the church could have saved that troubled young man. But the truth is, they didn't take the chance or see the need to try. They were too caught up in their own strife.

This tragic story is a haunting reminder to me that when the health and mission of the congregation hang in the balance (as well as the lives and eternal destinies of individuals), the overseer has a responsibility to protect the flock from division.

Again, the pastor or other staff minister does not have to be the one to do the confronting. It is often best for lay leaders in the church to handle such potentially explosive work. There will be times, however, when the responsibility for confrontation will fall to you. You should not shirk that.

Confrontation is more difficult for some of us, and meeting problems head-on is often not a strength of the "minister type." Nonetheless, leadership sometimes demands unpleasant confrontation. We must be discerning enough to know when to confront, courageous enough to do it when the situation demands it, and wise enough to know how.

If confrontation is your weakness, one thing you can do is to read some good books. Two I recommend are *Crucial Conversations: Tools for Talking When Stakes Are High*, by Kerry Patterson, Joseph Grenny, Ron McMillan, and Al Switzler, and *How to Have That Difficult Conversation You've Been Avoiding*, by Henry Cloud and John Townsend. Learn all you can, then muster your courage and have that hard talk.

Is Peace Possible with Everybody?

The Bible gives us clear instructions: "If it is possible, as far as it depends on you, live at peace with everyone" (Rom. 12:18). The verse clearly implies that peace with some people will be impossible.

I grew up near Fort McClellan in Anniston, Alabama. It is named for general George McClellan, a Union general from the "War Between the States." (Southerners wonder how that could have happened.) General McClellan, it seems, was rather irascible. Even President Abraham Lincoln had a hard time getting along with McClellan. Lincoln worked and worked with him, and went far beyond what most would have, in order to salvage his relationship with the general. When Lincoln gave him directives regarding the war, general McClellan became abrasive and disrespectful, even refusing to see the President when he was sitting in McClellan's home! Lincoln had enjoyed success with other men, such as William Seward and Edwin Stanton, with whom he, early on, had tense relationships. Lincoln was able to win over Seward and Stanton, despite their differences. Not so with McClellan. With all his efforts, McClellan proved stubbornly disrespectful. So Lincoln had to remove him from his post as commander of the Union army.[11] Lincoln was discouraged by his failure to bring McClellan around. But peace is not possible with everybody.

So What Do We Do with These People?

A friend of mine posted this on his Facebook page: "Mean-spirited church people...sometimes I'd just like to shoot 'em...bless their little hearts!" Well, gunfire is a bad idea. So what *can* we, *ought* we, *must* we do? Remember these words: "Warn a divisive person once, and then warn them a second time. After that, have nothing to do with them" (Titus 3:10). Moreover, God inspired Paul to write to the Christians in Rome: "I urge you, brothers and sisters, to watch out for those who cause divisions and put obstacles in your way that are contrary to the teaching you have learned. Keep away from them. For such people are not serving our Lord Christ, but their own appetites. By smooth talk and flattery they deceive the minds of naive people" (Rom. 16:17–18). Have nothing to do with them? Keep away from them? Those are strong words. And they're not *my* words.

How would Paul's counsel play out in the real world? Well, it seems that there should be at least some kind of formal censure from the church or church leadership, or a directive never to attend church conferences or business meetings. The fact that there is a new emphasis on "church discipline" in some circles means that, in many cases, a person would actually be invited to leave, and his or her name removed from the membership roll. There are some caveats, however, to keep in mind when contemplating punitive measures.

First, there is a fine line between fear and prudence, and between courage and hubris. As Richard Kriegbaum wrote in *Leadership Prayers*, "A brave fool cannot lead any better than a fearful sage can."[12] The choice not to take drastic measures might be the wise thing to do; it's not necessarily a sign of weakness. And the choice to censure or "discipline" someone might be an act of hubris, not righteous anger. We must constantly examine our motives, and let people who know and love us speak truth to us about what they believe is driving us.

Second, strength is in gentleness, not in retribution. Gentleness, according to its New Testament origins, is the intentional bridling or harnessing of our strength in order to defer to the needs of another. Gentleness is the strength of restraint.

But gentleness is not easy when people are acting foolishly.

One of my friends was asked by his church to leave a position in the corporate world to join the staff of his church. I asked his wife if he was going to consider it. "No way," she told me. "He doesn't suffer fools gladly." That rather odd phrase "suffer fools gladly" comes from the *King James* version of 2 Corinthians 11:19: "For ye suffer fools gladly, seeing ye yourselves are wise." Though Paul was probably speaking sarcastically there, it is true that the willingness and inner strength to put up with some nonsense once in a while makes for a more effective minister. So the wise minister understands that some maltreatment from people whom the Bible calls "foolish" comes with the territory. The wise and strong minister maintains his or her poise despite insensitive and offensive behavior and even when corrective measures are being taken.

I think my friend could have gone on that church staff and done well, by the way; but anyone who has ever been on a church staff understands why he wouldn't want to even try. Tolerating foolish behavior, while it comes with the territory, can wear one down.

Third, rare is the minister who is a completely innocent party in a church ruckus. It would be immoral to throw someone under the church bus when we are at least partially responsible for their poor behavior. If we cannot look the congregation in the eyes and say we wouldn't have done things differently, then we need to tap the brakes on our corrective measures. If we have contributed to the mess, let's back up, cool our jets, own our part, and wait. In due time disciplinary measures might be warranted despite our imperfect handling of the situation—but *only* in due time.

An Exception?

There might even be an exception to this be-a-pastor-to-all-the-people idea. I'm not talking about the typical troublemaker, the common complainer, or the everyday eccentric. I'm talking about people for whom "evil" seems to be the only fitting word. Or maybe "sociopath" or "vicious." Scott Peck encouraged us to recognize that the problem with some people is not just a crotchety disposition; the problem with some is the presence of evil. He noted further: "I have learned nothing in twenty years that would suggest that evil people can be rapidly influenced by any means other than raw power. They do not respond, at least in the short run, to either gentle kindness or any form of spiritual persuasion with which I am familiar."[13]

Look at these words from Acts 20:29: "I know that after I leave, savage wolves will come in among you and will not spare the flock." Those "wolves" are the ones G. Lloyd Rediger referred to as "Clergy Killers." In my work with churches, I've seen the bloody fingerprints of clergy killers on the clubs with which some fine ministers have been bludgeoned.

Olive branches don't work on die-hard troublemakers. Malicious detractors probably will not respond to kindness, no matter how noble your intentions. It seems to me that the only effective response to a clergy killer is to (1) document behavior, (2) marshal the powers available to you as the minister/pastor, and (3) intervene following Scripture's guidelines for the discipline of divisive members. That sometimes means denying the privilege of further participation in the church.

All Their Mugs (or at Least Most of Them)

On a mission trip a few summers ago, we worked at a church in Vermont with an interesting wall in their fellowship hall. On the wall of that small room were several mugs—coffee or hot chocolate mugs. We were curious enough to ask about them, and with great delight, one of the ladies of the church explained that each person brings his or her mug to church. When they have social gatherings, folks drink out of their personalized mugs, wash them, and hang them back on the wall. The wall is a beautiful mosaic of mugs, a kaleidoscope of cups, reflecting the varied interests and personalities of the church family. Not one flawless mug among them, I'm sure, but unique mugs, mugs that have stories behind them, mugs that represent something important to the owners. That wall has become a symbolic tapestry that represents the diversity of the church.

We had all kinds of "mugs" in the last church I served as pastor. We were becoming more ethnically diverse; we already were theologically diverse. We had folks from various generations, backgrounds, and perspectives. We allowed people to express their convictions by designating the missions portion of their contributions through a variety of channels. If we had had a mug wall, with mugs representing our differences, it would have been a medley of colors and shapes and sizes.

Our diversity was one of the church's greatest assets. Of course, that diversity was also one of our greatest dangers, and we had to be careful to nurture unity in our diversity. But at that church it works. I lived and ministered in a laboratory where it is confirmed that Christians of various stripes truly can get along.

There is, however, an occasional outlier—someone so destructive, divisive, and dangerous that he or she has to be dealt with sternly. In most cases, however, being shepherd to all the flock means being sure there is a place on the wall…and in our hearts… for all the mugs.

5

The Call

"...of which the Holy Spirit has made you..."

> *"[I]f I know God has called me to a particular place, I can be assured that what I bring is what the church must need. Is that outrageous? Arrogant? If I <u>didn't</u> believe that, I would call the moving van every time I'm struck by lightning. (The corollary, of course, is also true. If I find I can't do ministry the way God has called me to do it, then I must go elsewhere. And this for me is one test I use in determining when it's time to move on.)"*
>
> —Ben Patterson[1]

In the middle of my personal pastoral struggle years ago, I told my wife how bad things seemed to me. The tune I played her was gut-wrenching. Lesser spouses would have proclaimed with deep pity, "Honey, you've suffered enough. Why don't you quit and I'll support us. You take some time off and heal. Just go play golf." Not my wife. She said, "I'm ready for us to do whatever you think is best. Just look me in the eye and tell me that God is no longer calling you to be the pastor of this church."

I couldn't. So I remained in the proverbial saddle. Eventually, I became healthy, content, and on a roll—because I believed the Holy Spirit had put me there. I believed, to quote Paul in Acts 20:28, God's Spirit "made" me the pastor of that church. So I stayed until He made me something else. I'm so glad I stayed. The remaining years were my most productive. By the time I left, things were going so well it was really hard to walk away. I left the local church pastorate to do the ministry I'm doing now only because I had a profound sense that God was *making me* a different kind of minister.

What Paul referred to as the Holy Spirit "making you" is what we identify as the divine "call."

Importance of the Call

When agencies are evaluating potential missionaries, "the call" comes up often. Agency officials want to double and triple check the matter of a divine call when they are sending people to other cultures.

The call is critical for missionaries because they are going to be speaking in new tongues, discerning the nuances of a new culture, eating food that challenges their taste buds and digestive tracts, missing their families back home, and otherwise being subjected to new and unusual stresses. We know they are soon likely to wonder what they have gotten themselves into, so we want to know if they are truly called. We know they are going to need more than a sense of adventure to keep them on "the field." They're going to need to know they are there by divine appointment.

As we were preparing to leave for Nigeria, a missions leader said the following to our group of missionaries: "You're going to get your call out and hold it in your hand. You will turn it around and look at it from all angles. You will question it, probe it, and scrutinize it. You'd better be sure of it now, before you leave."

So what about ministers who happen to live in the country where they were born? Is there not the same critical need for a clear sense of call? Of course there is. Any ministers worth their salt are crossing barriers, learning new ways of communicating, and deciphering the culture—even in the land of their births!

As odd as it may seem, for those of us in the West, Christian ministry is harder than in many settings around the world. *Everyday life* elsewhere might be harder, particularly in regions where modern conveniences are rare. *Ministry*, however, is often easier for missionaries overseas than for pastors in the U.S. In some places outside of the Western world, people are encouragingly responsive and hold missionaries in high esteem. Also, some third-world cultures aren't changing nearly as fast as American culture is. And most missionaries in other lands spend most of their days doing front-line ministry instead of running "the machine" that the typical American church has become. So for those of us Westerners serving in the West, the divine call is even more important. Frankly, I've probed and scrutinized that call far more often in the U.S. than I did when we lived in Nigeria.

Still, regardless of where you were born, where you live now, or where you serve, you need to make sure that you are confident of your call. If you merely responded to the affirmations you received as a child from well-meaning Christian adults…or you entered vocational ministry with no more than a naïve sense of adventure…or you thought being a minister would compensate for some deep sense of spiritual inadequacy…then you do not have sufficient motivation to sustain you. You need to be sure of your call.

God's Decision, Not Mine

Dietrich Bonhoeffer wrote, "The choice of field for their labors does not depend on their own impulses or inclinations, but on where they are sent. This makes it quite clear that it is not their own work they are doing, but God's."[2] It is not ours to choose the field of labor, for this is not our work; it's God's.

Do you honestly believe you were *sent* to your present field of labor? Do you believe the Spirit of the Creator of the Universe made you the overseer of that congregation, or whatever you are doing wherever you are? If so, you have the foundation for an effective tenure. People with a deep and unshakable sense of call have a stickability that others do not.

In the book *So You Don't Want to Go to Church Anymore*, Bryce, a discouraged pastor, is considering leaving vocational ministry. He wonders if it's time to go, and his friend gives him some good advice:

> Part of the journey involves doing what he makes clear to you. If you've submitted it to him, then let him sort it out. If he were asking you to leave today, I think you'd know that, even in the face of your fears. If he hasn't made it clear to you then wait. Just keep loving him and following him every day. I'm learning the joy of resting in him, doing what I know to do and not doing what I don't know to do…
>
> "This is His decision, not yours, and it will be clear when it is clear.[3]

This—going or staying—really ought to be God's decision. It's a matter of call. And here is my definition of "call": **Call is the ongoing promptings of God's Spirit, confirmed through Scripture, the faith community, intellect, and experience, that communicate** *"These are your roles in my mission."* Let's unpack that briefly.

First, call is ongoing, not something that we deal with and move on. As long as we are following Jesus, the call is always developing, always unfolding.

Second, call is a "prompting," a mystical, supernatural sense that the Creator of the universe has called my name and nudged me toward something.

Third, to talk about "promptings" is somewhat dangerous, for I can tell myself that God has "prompted" me when, in actuality, I am merely following my own aspirations. So we need checks and balances. Those checks and balances are Scripture (God is not going to contradict His written word with personal words to you), input from fellow believers (who know the truth about us and love us enough to tell us the truth), intellect (the mind is a terrible thing to waste), and experience (the more experiences I have, the more I understand myself and, perhaps in small ways, the heart of God).

Fourth, God's call is to roles, not merely to a role. God's "will" has to do with more than where I live or what I do. God's will for me includes my entire existence. Remember Romans 12:1: "Take your everyday, ordinary life—your sleeping, eating, going-to-work, and walking-around life—and place it before God as an offering" (The Message).

Finally, it is critical that we never think this is *our* mission. We are simply joining God in *His* mission. Since the 1960s we've been talking about the Missio Dei, the mission of God. We do that not just because we want to sound erudite; the term actually helps us remember that the mission of which we speak is not ours; it's God's. God's purposes for us always fit within His plan for His people and His world. It's not about us.

Confirming the Call

How do I know if the Holy Spirit made me (called me to be) a minister at this place at this time?

Anytime sinful, finite humans are trying to discern the will and ways of our Creator, the process will be shrouded in mystery. *Mysterious*, however, is not synonymous with *impossible*. We can have enough light to see the path ahead. We can be confident about our call—so confident that we can weather storms, confusion, disappointment, and our own inevitable missteps. I believe we can know whether or not the Spirit has "made us" (called us to be) in a specific ministry position.

A "COMPASS"

Here I offer COMPASS as a tool for discernment. This human tool is not intended to supplant, but rather to complement, your practice of spiritual disciplines and your sincere desire to hear God. When I say COMPASS I'm talking about a process that uses a combination of practices that have helped me discern the voice of the Spirit: *Constancy, Observation by Others, Motive, Peculiar Passions, Aptitudes, Seasoning, Sensible Decision-Making*.[4] Let me walk you through this process.

C – Constancy

Opportunities and ideas might come along fairly often for you. Perhaps you will be energized by new possibilities, intrigued by novel trends, and flattered by inquiries from other churches. So you must be able to discern whether or not the idea or opportunity is merely a fleeting enticement.

The test of time will help you with your discernment. If, after weeks, you still are being dogged by the thought, then perhaps you should take it seriously. If, after some time, you can't shake the hunch that you should take a step toward this opportunity, it might be that you actually should do so. Maybe the Spirit is up to something.

The young assistant Samuel and the priest Eli recognized that God was calling Samuel only after the fourth occurrence of God speaking to the young man. It was the persistence of that voice— the unrelenting nature of God's call—which gave them a clue that Samuel's unsettledness was the result of something besides Samuel's spicy dinner the evening before. God, in fact, was calling.

If God wants you somewhere, He won't let go of you. Let His persistence be your confirmation.

O – Observation by Others

I cannot tell you how important it is to hear from people who know us well and love us enough to speak candidly to us. I have followed a model that I found in Richard Foster's book *Celebration of Discipline*. He calls it "meetings for clearness,"[5] and it simply means getting a group of Christian friends together to pray and to talk as a group about the matter at hand. The one in need of clarity has to give permission to his or her circle of advisors for them to speak candidly. I've done this twice, including in my decision whether to remain in the pastorate or take a new ministry role, and it has been very helpful.

Letting people you trust and who have your best interest at heart speak into your decision is wise. Remember, "Plans fail for lack of counsel, / but with many advisers they succeed" (Prov. 15:22).

M – Motive

I loved being a football player. I just wasn't very good at it. When I was in the tenth grade, I found myself riding the proverbial pine—sitting on the bench watching others play. My ego couldn't stand it, so I decided to quit. Because quitting outright would have been embarrassing, I decided to play the "will of God" card. I went into the office of the late Coach Farrell and announced rather matter-of-factly that it was God's will for me to quit the team. Nearly four decades later I still can quote his response to me word for word: "Son, I'm sure you know a lot more about that kind of thing than I do. But I wouldn't want us to blame something on God that He didn't have anything to do with."

Busted.

Since that humiliating day I've tried not to hide behind, or otherwise adulterate, the "will of God." So I have to check my motives often when I have a decision to make. Since I can justify and rationalize self-serving decisions with little effort, I must be self-aware and unwilling to deceive myself if I am going to hear clearly from the Lord.

Motives for leaving our present role and moving to another can easily get mixed, of course. But so can our motives for *not* leaving. Are we just drawing a paycheck? Too comfortable to step out in faith to do something else?

Whether it's a matter of going or staying, it's critical that we examine our motives.

P – Peculiar Passions

The body of Christ is beautifully diverse. Our individual peculiarities add both value to the Church and clarity to our calls. God is going to call us to those things for which he wired us. Our unique gifts and passions—and whether or not a ministry opportunity fits those gifts and passions—help us discern how and where to find our places in God's mission to the world. Often if something *feels* right, it *is* right. God does often give you the desires of your heart (Ps. 20:4; 37:4).

A – Aptitudes

God inspired Peter to write, "Each of you should use whatever gift you have received to serve others, as faithful stewards of God's grace in its various forms… If anyone serves, they should do so with the strength God provides" (1 Pet. 4:10–11). Scripture also says, "[L]et's just go ahead and be what we were made to be" (Rom. 12:6, *The Message*).

So, without belaboring the point, you and I simply have to be honest about our abilities and interests, and ask whether our present or potential ministry positions actually fit them. That's not to say that we ought to avoid opportunities to grow or stretch. Ministry often demands that we develop new skills or significantly strengthen present skills. However, we cannot be someone we are not. If we are violating our identity in order to serve in a particular place, that's probably the wrong place for us to be. Joy and effectiveness are in roles that fit.

S – Seasoning

In 1 Timothy 3, the Bible warns new believers not to take on roles for which they are not ready. A certain seasoning is necessary for each level of our growth.

Over twenty years ago, I asked an influential pastor to recommend me to a certain position. It was a dream role, and that man's blessing would have given me a leg up over the other candidates. But he chose not to recommend me. He said I wasn't yet ready for it.

I was insulted and hurt. Now, however, I know he was right. I know now that I was not ready for that role at the time. That ship soon sailed into rough waters, and I sincerely believe that it would have been catastrophic had I been at the helm. The ship would have sunk, and I would have either gone down with that ship or been lost at sea.

Taking on more than we're ready for is unhealthy all around.

However, if God has prepared us for greater influence and responsibility, then being open to that is a good thing. That same man who refused to recommend me (I'll call him "Bill") once advised another minister in our area to leave! That other minister was in a small church and content as he could be. His role was comfortable, affirming, and safe. Bill had recommended the pastor of that small church to some other larger churches, but the pastor of that small church had refused to be considered. Now, you might be thinking it was admirable for that fellow to remain in that little church. And perhaps it was. Or maybe—as Bill put it—maybe that pastor in the comfortable, affirming, safe setting was scared, lazy, or otherwise unwilling to take on a more challenging role.

I am not implying that a bigger church, higher profile, or larger salary should be our goal. Very often, turning down a more lucrative position is a sign of right priorities. Just make sure, though, that the fear of change and the comfort of the familiar don't keep you away from bigger roles to which God might be calling you. There is no honor in simply remaining at the same level and coasting.

S – Sensible Decision-making

Human judgment is faulty. But so are weather forecasts. We ought not completely ignore either one.

Gathering information and using the gray matter with which God blessed us is a legitimate and necessary part of the discernment process. Gather all the data you can gather. Know all the details you can know. Turn over every rock you can turn over.

Though we walk by faith and not by sight, it still makes good sense for us to do our best not to walk off cliffs.

A Lifetime Call?

I am not among those who believe a call to vocational ministry is necessarily a lifetime call. I believe you have every right to re-examine your call from time to time—to take it out and evaluate it. Of course, walking away from a call to vocational ministry is a serious thing; it should be done only after significant wrestling with one's self and with God. It's sobering to think one might casually abandon a vocational role in God's mission. Yet, I still contend that one need not feel ashamed if one truly believes God's calling on his or her life has shifted away from vocational ministry.

Leaving vs. Staying

You should stay until the Holy Spirit makes you (calls you to be) something somewhere else.

In his book *Seven Things They Don't Teach You in Seminary*, John Killinger captured the tension between needing to go and leaving too quickly. He acknowledged:

> Sometimes…it becomes necessary for a minister to leave and locate in another church that is more civil or more hospitable. Ernest Campbell, of New York's Riverside Church, said in a sermon that shaking the dust off our feet, which Jesus advised when certain villages didn't accept the teaching of his Apostles, ought to have been made a sacrament, something accorded the status of a holy necessity.

Thus there are occasions when stubbornly remaining at a church, to quote Killinger, "would be a disservice to everybody, including God." In fact, some "may well discover that dealing with the local church has a dampening effect on our souls that would be spiritually fatal were we to continue in it for long."[6]

My friend, Randy Ashcraft, once told me a great story about water skiing. His brother, the driver of the boat, was giving instructions to his sister, who was bobbing in the water with her two skis pointed skyward. She was trying to ski for the first time. Among other words of advice, the brother said, "Whatever happens, don't let go of the rope!"

If you have learned to water ski, you know the wisdom of that advice. If you let go of the rope too quickly and are unwilling to press on through the wall of water coming toward you, you never will learn to ski.

So the brother hit the boat's throttle, the rope tightened, and the sister began the difficult task of "coming up" above the water.

After a few seconds, she fell. And she remembered her brother's advice: "Whatever happens, don't let go of the rope." So for some painful seconds, with Randy looking on in deep concern, she hung tenaciously onto the rope. *She's going to drown!* Randy thought, as the water beat her and threw her around. Then, mercifully, the rope was jerked from her white-knuckled hands.

Randy's moral of the story is that sometimes a refusal to let go of the rope is just crazy. You could drown. Or the rope could get jerked painfully from your unwilling hands. Sometimes you've just got to let go of the rope. That's true in vocational ministry as well.

Of course, knowing when to let go of the role or position you are in is not easy. Consider John Killinger's comments: "It would be easy to walk away like spoiled children who don't like the way the game is going—to take our few marbles and go somewhere to play by ourselves. Sticking it out—turning things around, making lemonade out of the lemons—may be God's calling to some of us."[7]

If you believe yourself to have been *hired*, then resigning is a viable escape. If you believe yourself to have been *called*, however, the very thought of not remaining in that role is formidable. Such a decision is not taken lightly. Like the words of the wedding ceremony, acceptance of a call is made "soberly, reverently and in the fear of God." Such decisions are not set aside lightly or easily.

Eugene Peterson's words from *Under the Unpredictable Plant* are worth including here. Peterson warns that "every time a pastor abandons one congregation for another out of boredom or anger or restlessness, the pastoral vocation of all of us is vitiated." And he illustrates:

> It was not unusual for monks to leave one monastery and set out for another, supposing themselves to be responding to a greater challenge, attempting a more austere holiness. But these quests were always a little suspect: was it really more of God they were after, or were they avoiding the God who was revealing himself to them?
>
> By Benedict's time this restlessness disguised as spiritual questing was widespread. When the monastery in which the monks were living proved less than ideal, they typically went looking for a better one with a holier abbot or prioress and more righteous brothers and sisters. They

were sure that if they just got into the right community they could have a most effective ministry. And Benedict put a stop to it. He introduced the vow of stability: stay where you are.[8]

Peterson, like Killinger, doesn't ignore the inevitable need and legitimate call that some have to move to another place of ministry. Yet he contends:

> [T]he norm for pastoral work is stability. Twenty-, thirty-, and forty-year-long pastorates should be typical among us (as they once were) and not exceptional. Far too many pastors change parishes out of adolescent boredom, not as a consequence of mature wisdom. When this happens, neither pastors nor congregations have access to the conditions that are hospitable to maturity in the faith.[9]

Often the easy response to boredom, conflict, or a dry spell is to leave. But as with marriage, when you're committed to staying, you will take steps you otherwise would not take.

When you cannot say that the Spirit has rescinded His call, and when you are unwilling to leave until He does, then you learn to do ministry differently. You're more patient with yourself. You relate to those around you more graciously. You stop fantasizing about how good your life would be if you could just go somewhere else. You refuse just to pack up your marbles and leave.

Let's return to the monk theme that Eugene Peterson discusses. The desert fathers were monks who left "civilization" to go live in Middle Eastern deserts as early as the third century. One of those holy men, Abba Anthony, once was asked, "What must one do to please God?" Abba Anthony gave answers that we'd expect, such as, "Be aware of God's presence," and, "Obey God's word." But his third piece of sage advice was this: "Wherever you find yourself—do not easily leave."[10] Do not easily leave. That's wise advice.

Leaving is sometimes attractive, isn't it? Just walking away. Finding greener grass. Going to where the people are easier to work with. Leaving, however, is most often not the answer.

The missionary Paul began one of his letters to his protégé Timothy with an interesting mandate: "As I urged you when I went into Macedonia, stay there in Ephesus" (1 Tim. 1:3a). Timothy was young at the time and perhaps easily discouraged. There certainly were plenty of things to be discouraged about in Ephesus, and the people Timothy led were his biggest problem. The Ephesian church was a somewhat troublesome group of relatively new and spiritually immature Christians. Many had wild and heretical beliefs, for the influence of idol worship was strong in that church. Many were also skeptical of Timothy's leadership abilities. Because of his youth and inexperience and because he had the difficult task of following that superb leader named Paul, the folks at Ephesus apparently were looking down their noses at Timothy (1 Tim. 4:12; 2 Tim. 2:6–8). Perhaps Timothy had expressed openly to Paul his desire to leave those recalcitrant malcontents—to move to greener pastures—to go to an easier assignment where the people were good-humored. But Paul said, "Timothy, you stay in Ephesus."

So how do we know when, or if, it's time to let go of the rope? Maybe these questions will help:

- *Is your family hurting?*
- *Is your physical, spiritual, and emotional well-being in jeopardy (I don't mean, "Are you disappointed?" I'm talking about a long-lasting, deep pain that jeopardizes your soul.)*
- *Can you look in the mirror and into the eyes of your spouse or close friends and say, "God has released me"?*
- *Have the leaders lost their confidence and trust in you, and is that confidence and trust not regainable?*
- *Are you having to violate your integrity and identity in order to stay?*
- *Is your heart long since not in this anymore?*
- *Is the God-given vision dead?*
- *Is it simply a bad fit? Do your skill sets, passions, and gifts no longer match the needs of the organization? It could be that the church has outgrown your skill sets, passions, and gifts, or vice versa. Or it could be that you and the search team just missed on the fit. Bad fits can be the result of several factors and might be no one's fault.*
- *Do those who love you, and whose opinions you trust, say they think you should consider leaving?*
- *Has God given you a vision that can be fulfilled only if you leave to serve in another place and/or role?*

I shared this list one night with a room full of pastors. One pastor raised his hand and asked, "So how many of those do you need to check before you know it's time to go?" It was a great question. I think the answer is two-fold.

First, ask yourself how many of those ten check points are true for you. In other words, how many of them did you say yes to?

Second, determine the level to which each is true. For example, on the question, "Is your family hurting?" would you say your family members have merely expressed sadness and disappointment over the conflicts at church? Or does the pain run deeper than that? Would you, for example, say that the tense church situation has caused at least one family member to be deeply depressed, significantly afraid, or otherwise in great distress?

And on the question, "Have the leaders lost their confidence in you?" would you say you simply made a bad decision that disappointed them, but they still trust your heart and your otherwise good track record so they are giving you the benefit of the doubt? Or has the situation reached the stage that significant leaders are saying, "We can and will no longer support you"?

I realize this is not a scientific survey, but once you start considering how many of those check points apply to you and you ask yourself at what level each one applies, perhaps an answer about leaving will emerge. You will come to know that it's time to drop the rope or keep hanging on.

There was a stretch during my last pastorate when I was clearly taking on water. I felt myself going under. I was tempted to let go of the rope. But I didn't, mainly because my wife told me to look her in the eye and tell her that God was finished with me in that place. That I could not say. So I hung on to the rope. And then I "came up," as it were. I emerged from that difficult time to enjoy a wonderfully fruitful and joyful period. The spirit, attendance, giving, growth—the typical measurements of a church's health— were wonderful. And when the opportunity to do something different (working for Fresh Expressions US and consulting with churches) came, I was able to let go of the rope simply because it was the right timing, not because I feared drowning.

If you have water skied, you will know how good it feels to come up out of the water, ski until you're tired, and then, at the point of your choosing, let go of the rope and gently sink into the water. Or, better yet, you let go of the rope as the boat whips you toward the dock and you gently glide, then sink, right there in front of your friends and family. "It's time for someone else to take a turn," you say, and you enjoy the sweet rest that follows a successful tow around the lake.

That's what it felt like for me. At one point I was barely hanging on to the rope and tempted to let go. But because I didn't let go, because I hung on, God in His grace allowed me to "come up out of the water" and enjoy some really rewarding years. Then, when the time was right (and I admit I was feeling a cumulative weariness), I was able to drop the rope, glide gently into the shallow waters around the dock, and grab another rope that seemed much better suited for me.

I know that not every ministerial situation has such a good and rewarding ending, even when we know we are doing God's will. All I'm saying is that, sometimes, even when it feels like we should move on, staying may be the better course.

Not Yet and "Nevertheless"

Somewhere I heard that the answer to the question, "When should I leave?" is, "Not yet." I'm convinced that is indeed the answer until the Spirit asks you to leave. If He hasn't said, "Go," then I believe you should stay until, and if, He ever does release you. Remember: Do not easily leave.

On April 14, 1957, in Montgomery's Dexter Avenue Baptist Church, Martin Luther King, Jr. preached a sermon about Jesus' painful prayer in the Garden of Gethsemane: "Let this cup pass from me, *nevertheless*, let your will be done." King was building on the theme developed earlier by Harry Emerson Fosdick, and what King said about that "nevertheless" has had a deep impact on me. King said that what we do with that "nevertheless" is the test of our character and devotion to God:

> This, you see, is the central test of an individual's life…
> How one moves out from "let this cup pass from me" to
> "nevertheless." This determines your life. This determines
> how you will live it… Few people learn the lesson. And they
> end up in all of the misery and all of the agony and all of the
> frustration of life because they can't quite jump from one
> to the other. They live on "let this cup pass from me." And
> they try to, when they see that the cup is still there, they try
> to get away from it through diverse methods and manners.

And they end up more frustrated. They try the method of escapism... One must learn to make the transition from "let this cup pass from me" to "nevertheless, not my will, but Thy will be done."[11]

I have learned that when I try to manipulate some form of escape, when I manufacture some way out on my own, I just end up with *different* problems. There is no shame in praying, "God, deliver me from this situation," as long as we're willing to pray, "Nevertheless, I trust your judgment better than my own, so I submit to Your plan even if that means I suffer this trial." Remember God's word to us through James: "Let perseverance finish its work so that you may be mature and complete, not lacking anything... Blessed is the one who perseveres under trial (1:4, 12a). Trials, responded to appropriately, make us mature and complete, the complete package. But notice that trials alone do not produce maturity; it is the trials *responded to appropriately.*

Another way to look at this is found in Ruth Haley Barton's helpful book *Pursuing God's Will Together*. Barton speaks of "the prayer for indifference."

> The first and most essential dynamic of discernment is the movement toward indifference. In the context of spiritual discernment, indifference is a positive term signifying that "I am indifferent to anything but God's will." This is "interior freedom" or a state of openness to God in which we are free from undue attachment to any particular outcome. There is a capacity to relinquish whatever might keep us from choosing God and love, and we have come to a place where we want God and God's will more than anything—more than ego gratification, more than wanting to look good in the eyes of others, more than personal ownership, comfort or advantage.[12]

Some of the most important words you can declare, then, are "not yet" and "nevertheless." A willingness to say those words will prevent impulsive, unwise decisions.

Faith vs. Scheming

Faith, in the words of Warren Wiersbe, "is living without scheming."[13] "Scheming" here means orchestrating events in one's favor—devising plans that "help" God fulfill His plans for us.

Of course, there is a fine line between making oneself available and manipulating things. There is certainly no sin in letting people know you are open to a new position. However, once you make your availability known, then trust God with the process. Don't prod. Don't stir the pot. Don't work the system. Don't try to rig the ending. God doesn't need our help in fulfilling His plans for our lives. When we interfere, when we try too hard to help God out, we tend to mess things up.

Faith means waiting for God to accomplish what only He can accomplish, without rushing ahead and trying to pull strings or otherwise orchestrate the outcome. Hebrews 6:12 says that it is through "faith and patience" that we "inherit what has been promised." Faith is living without scheming.

Never Cut Down a Tree in the Wintertime

In his famous book *Tough Times Never Last, But Tough People Do,* Robert Schuller wrote that when he was a boy, on a cold winter day his family needed some firewood. So his dad found a dead tree and cut it down. In the spring, much to his dismay, new shoots sprouted around the trunk. Schuller's father had thought for sure he had cut down a dead and worthless tree. After all, the leaves were all gone; the limbs snapped as if the old tree was dead. But he learned that despite the tree's appearance, it was not dead. It was winter! There was still life at the old taproot. He then said to his son Robert: "Bob, don't ever forget this important lesson. Never cut down a tree in the wintertime. Never make a negative decision in the low time. Never make your most important decisions when you are in your worst mood. Wait. Be patient. The storm will pass. The spring will come."[14]

To cut down trees in the wintertime—to make decisions when you are so ticked off, hurt, or discouraged that you can't think straight—is poor decision-making.

Have You Been to Your Bethel Lately?

As we read in Genesis 35:1, God said to Jacob, "Go up to Bethel and settle there, and build an altar there to God, who appeared to you when you were fleeing from your brother Esau." Jacob did go back to Bethel—back to the sacred place where he had seen the vision of the ladder and to which God had directed him. God again appeared and confirmed that Jacob now would be known as "Israel." Bethel would forever be the defining place for him—

the site where he met God twice—the hallowed ground where a merciful God chose to bless a sinful man with a special place in God's mission to the world.

Have you been to your Bethel lately?

Ted Traylor wrote a moving story about a particularly difficult stretch in his leadership as a pastor. He described a "three-hour barrage of insults and accusations" during a church business meeting. Ted's wife was targeted, too, and the church he loved was being demonized in the community. Ted hated going to work and admitted he would have gone to "Toadsuck, Arkansas," if God would just have provided a way out of his painful situation. But, as Ted wrote, "Why is it you never hear from a (search) committee when you need one?"

Then one night three of his close friends showed up unannounced at his house. They had been on a "road trip" that day. They had traveled to Ted's home place in Pisgah, Alabama. His friends had heard Ted talk about the rock on the mountain where he would go and pray as a young "preacher boy." There on that rock young Ted had practiced his earliest sermons. There on that rock Ted had spent hours discerning God's voice. One of those friends reached out and handed Ted two large chunks of that rock. They had busted pieces off the rock upon which Ted had received his call. Ted took those chunks of rock and planted them in the side yard. Now he sometimes stands on them, remembering the God who called him.[15]

You might need to find your rock—that place, that event, that moment or those moments—when your part in the plan of the Creator became clear. A spiritual journey back to your original call might give you enough strength to stay where you are.

My personal Bethel is a street in downtown Caracas. But not everyone has a physical Bethel, although all vocational ministers (I hope) have a "spiritual Bethel"—a time in life, perhaps an unfolding process—during which we believed the Creator of the universe was laying His hand on us. Returning to that from time to time is important. Write it down. Replay it. Don't let that memory die.

One More Word

When I was struggling with near burnout, I read Gordon MacDonald's *Who Stole My Church?* One of the most helpful insights from that book was this: You probably are tempted to leave that tradition-bound, stuck-in-the-mud church you're in and go off and plant a new congregation. And church planting is an honorable effort. But maybe you ought to stay where you are. Maybe you ought to "be patient, be prayerful, seek allies, build alliances with other generations." If so, with time, "you just may see a miracle—a hundred-year-old church that acts with the spirit of an enthusiastic teenager."[16] That was what I did, and by God's grace, in the years following that decision, God did some absolutely amazing things in and through our church. If I'd left at my low time, I would have left prematurely and missed out on some of the things that I remember with the greatest joy.

Don't leave until you give the church one more opportunity to act like an effervescent, irrepressible teenager.

6

Overseers with Authority

"...the Holy Spirit has made you overseers..."

There must be systems and safeguards. This is true, but it is still an interesting phenomenon to lead without the authority to lead. All leadership should be conditional otherwise there is no accountability. But in so many of our churches major decisions are made at meetings that might not adequately represent the whole church family. I have never been power hungry or have sought authority, but I can't help feeling worn down by a system that asked me to lead but never really freed me up to do my best.

—STEVE BAGI, PASTORPAIN[1]

The word translated "overseers" in Acts 20:28 is the Greek word *episkopos*, sometimes translated "bishops." Remember that Acts 20:17 tells us that Paul gathered the "elders" (*presbyterous*) of the church. As recorded in verse 28, when Paul spoke to the elders (*presbyterous*), he addressed them as "overseers" (*episkopos*) and "shepherds" (*poimainein*, "pastors"). I believe the three terms—elder, overseer, and shepherds—were interchangeable and synonymous terms in Paul's world. They were references to and descriptions of the role we call "minister" or "pastor." No matter one's position on these titles and offices, it is important for all of us not to lose any one of those terms—elder, overseer, and shepherd—as we consider the authority and responsibility of the vocational minister in the church.

I'll talk about the shepherding aspect of our role in the next chapter. Here I am going to talk about what it means to be the overseer of a congregation. This is probably the one place where the role of senior (or lead) pastor and the role of other staff ministers differ somewhat. While each minister on a church staff oversees certain areas of ministry, it is my understanding that one person—the senior pastor, or whatever the corresponding term is in your tradition—is responsible for general oversight of the congregation. That person is the spiritual overseer of the church.

Yet, no matter what your ministerial role, if you have experienced a divine call to vocational ministry, remember:

- You are not a lackey; you are an overseer, a leader.
- You are not primarily a doer; you are an overseer. (Ephesians 4:12 says you are to "equip his (God's) people for works of service."
- You are not someone's private chaplain; you are an overseer.

Shepherds Who Oversee and Overseers Who Shepherd

I don't want to get ahead of myself, because I'm going to talk about "shepherding" in the next chapter. But we can't put that topic off completely, for how we "shepherd" will determine how we "oversee." And we have to do both simultaneously. First Peter 5:1–4 explores this dual role of shepherd and overseer, servant and leader:

> To the elders among you, I appeal as a fellow elder and a witness of Christ's sufferings who also will share in the glory to be revealed: Be shepherds of God's flock that is under your care, serving as overseers—not because you must, but because you are willing, as God wants you to be; not pursuing dishonest gain, but eager to serve; not lording it over those entrusted to you, but being examples to the flock. And when the Chief Shepherd appears, you will receive the crown of glory that will never fade away.

So, as we proceed through this chapter, keep the shepherd image in the back of your mind. Spiritual overseers are not military generals or even benevolent dictators. They are overseers who shepherd, and shepherds who oversee.

We will have to be careful not to soft-pedal this matter of oversight, however. Authori*tarian* leadership (the pastor is boss) should be rejected. However, authori*tative* leadership (the pastor speaks and lives with contagious conviction and vision) is the kind of leadership that results in the advance of God's Kingdom. If our churches are to be effective, they must have strong leadership. Tentative leaders often allow their churches to sink into quagmires from which teams of oxen couldn't drag them.

Spiritual Authority Is Unquestionable

Titus 2:15b says, "Encourage and rebuke with all authority. Do not let anyone despise you." God was speaking through Paul to Titus about Titus' authority, and he wrote knowing his words would be read in public among the Christians in Crete. So Paul was subtly reminding both Titus and the congregation of the spiritual authority that came with Titus' calling.

In Acts 15 we find the story of the first big church fight and a great example of what leading with spiritual authority looks like. When push came to shove, it was James, not a committee, making the call about the controversy. James heard the various perspectives, and then declared that the Church would respect the Jewish tradition out of which they'd grown but would not be hampered by traditionalism. The pastor assumed oversight. He didn't poll anyone. He said, "Here's what we're gonna do."

What James did is echoed in 1 Timothy 5:17. This text says that elders are supposed to "direct the affairs of the church." Notice: it does not say "dictate the details of the church," nor does it say "bow to the church's traditions and genuflect to its strong personalities."

"Directing the affairs of the church" has to mean, among other things, general oversight of operations. The congregation cannot vote every time a decision has to be made; decisions have to be entrusted to church leaders. In practice today, most elders or ministers would be granted the responsibility and authority for day-to-day operations and would be expected to refer the big matters—budgets, calling a senior pastor, doctrinal statements, transfer of property, and the like—to the congregation, bishop, or another denominational leadership, depending on the church's polity.

Yet, "directing the affairs" almost certainly has to do with more than day-to-day operations. When the Greek widows were not receiving the appropriate ministry from their Jerusalem church, for example, the elders (apostles) decided how the church would ensure fair distribution of food. It was assumed they had the authority to make calls like that. This is where the polity of various traditions, as well as the history and culture of individual churches, comes into play. Nevertheless, whatever specifics Paul had in mind when he wrote 1Timothy 5:17 ("The elders who direct the affairs of the church well are worthy of double honor, especially those whose work is preaching and teaching"), it is obvious that the vocational minister called to oversight of a congregation is more than a hired hand.

Authority and the Priesthood of Believers

How do we balance, "Everybody's a priest," and, "Submit to your spiritual authorities"?

The spiritual authority of leaders is tempered by what we Protestants call the priesthood of believers. Since, by virtue of our relationship with God through Jesus, all Christ-followers are priests, then the Reverends are not the only ones who can hear from God, interpret Scripture and minister to the people. How does this biblical fact fit in with all else we have been talking about in regard to those of us in vocational ministry? In practice, a clash sometimes occurs. I read somewhere that pastors like invoking the priesthood of believers when church members are getting lazy, and church members like invoking the priesthood of believers when pastors are getting uppity. But how is this *supposed* to work? How does the message that we all are priests (1 Pet. 2:5, 9; Rev. 5:10) inform our understanding of ministerial oversight?

In the New Testament there is a balance of power between the pastor and the congregation. On the one hand, the Bible speaks of the spiritual authority of the pastor:

- "Have confidence in your leaders and submit to their authority, because they keep watch over you as those who must give an account. Do this so that their work will be a

joy, not a burden, for that would be of no benefit to you."
(Heb. 13:17)

- "Now we ask you, brothers and sisters, to acknowledge those who work hard among you, who care for you in the Lord and who admonish you." (1 Thess. 5: 12)

On the other hand, the Bible speaks of the personal responsibility and freedom of the believer:

- "Now the Berean Jews were of more noble character than those in Thessalonica, for they received the message with great eagerness and examined the Scriptures every day to see if what Paul said was true." (Acts 17:11)

So there is this dance that we do—balancing the pastor's spiritual authority with each believer's responsibility and freedom. How we conduct that dance is, frankly, situational. There is no rule applicable in every circumstance, and as long as we hold in tension these rather paradoxical truths, we are being true to the biblical prescription for our relationship.

Of course, we all know that in every congregation there are *priests* and there are *Priests*. In other words, some of the members of your church hold greater influence than others. As hard as it is to admit it, in some churches those Priests hold more influence than the pastor does. So, you will be a more effective overseer if you will figure out who the recognized influencers are and get them on board. You obviously must seek the input, advice, and support for important initiatives from those whose voices carry lots of weight. You don't boss those folks, or anyone else in the congregation, around.

Nevertheless—and please hear me on this—when you're speaking to those influencers, speak as the church's overseer, not as one lower down the food chain than they. Don't pander and don't grovel. With your calling came spiritual authority.

You are not the only one in church to whom the Spirit speaks, so be a good listener. People in the congregation can thwart your purposes; they can even fire you. Nevertheless, before God you will be held responsible for the congregation and how you led them (Hebrews 13:17), so lead with confidence. We again turn to the veteran Bill Self for help on this aspect of pastoral leadership and the priesthood of believers:

The priesthood of believers was never intended to cause the church to be led from the middle, nor was it meant to unpriest the priest or the one qualified to preach, lead, and cast the vision... This is not a plea for pastoral tyranny, but rather a plea for vocational decisiveness and assertiveness. More churches are hurt by pastoral default than have ever been hurt by pastoral domination... Too many pastors believe that they should lead, if they lead at all, not from the balls of their feet but from the back of their heels... Of course there are times when the pastor must compromise; we are not masters of the universe. Nevertheless, the leader's first task is to sound the trumpet clear and loud. He should not give an uncertain sound.[2]

When the chips are down and a decisive voice is needed, it is needed badly. Of course the chips aren't always down, and overplaying the "we need a decisive leader" card is unwise. But most lay priests appreciate overseers who offer courageous, principled, unfaltering leadership.

One area in which the overseer has the greatest role to play is in the discerning of God's vision. Nothing is more important to your congregation than a God-given vision, and I believe the primary (not sole) conduit for that vision is the overseer. That vision should neither be relegated by the pastor to others nor determined by him or her in isolation. It is to God that the pastor will answer for how well the congregation followed God's promptings, but it is to that very congregation that the pastor must turn for confirmation of the vision, collaboration in refining the vision, and correction of the course along the way. In fact, it is best when the vision is discerned organically, with the full congregation involved and the trusted overseer speaking into that process of discernment. His or her voice should not be the driving force, but it does need to be the most important voice in the vision discussion.

"...with many advisors"

People love to advise their ministers. How we respond to that advice will help shape our leadership and determine the level of authority that people will grant us. If we flippantly disregard advice, we will soon find ourselves flippantly disregarded by the ones we are charged to oversee. However, if we want so badly to be liked that we follow *all* the advice we get, we will appear more like pinballs than leaders.

Furthermore, every person's interpretation of things should not be weighed equally. While we are all priests, we all should not have the same clout in the church. In fact, J. Oswald Sanders warned the pastor to "resist the idea of 'leadership from the rear.'" He noted that it was "leadership from the rear" that got the people of Israel stuck in the wilderness.[3] Numbers 32 tells us that naysayers, not forward-thinkers, were allowed to chart the Israelites' course. People who walked by sight, not by faith, kept the people of Israel out of the Promised Land for forty years. We can't let that happen to our churches.

Part of our responsibility is to distinguish the spiritual voices from the unspiritual ones. Having plenty of advisors comes divinely recommended (Prov. 15:22). Accepting the advice of every advisor, however, is not advisable!

Protestant Churches and Spiritual Oversight: A Peculiar Problem?

Do Protestant churches have a particular problem with spiritual oversight? Joseph Girzone, a former Catholic priest, had an interesting take on this in his book *Joshua*:

> [T]he priest spoke and agreed that priests exist to serve the people, but they, too, frequently would rather rule them instead. Unfortunately, people tolerate this because they are afraid of incurring the priest's wrath. The problem seems to be just the opposite with the Protestant churches. There the problem ministers face is too much control by the people, so the minister is often afraid to preach the real message of Jesus and compromises his ministry so he can keep his job.[4]

I can't speak to whether or not my Roman Catholic friends are afraid of their priests, but this idea of Protestant ministers being under the thumb of the people is an intriguing observation.

A Catholic friend and I were sitting on my deck one evening talking things over, and he said: "I don't get it with you Baptists. In my church, we assume that the guy who's been to seminary and has years of experience and lives with church matters day in and day out knows what he's doing. In Baptist churches [and he knows lots of Baptists] people in the pew assume they know more about running a church than the professional does!"

Are he and Girzone on to something? Peter L. Steinke, who works primarily with Protestant churches, may have put his finger on an expectation of the minister that characterizes Protestant church members in particular: "Remember, you [the minister] are not authorized to push us, quiz us, or surprise us. If you want to be liked, don't get ahead of us. Be our leader, but keep following us."[5]

Once I was at a dinner attended by members of churches across the city, and I happened to sit at the table with three couples, all of whom were members of the same country club. I listened as they talked about the staff of their club. There was an undeniable tone to their complaints: in the minds of these club members, the staff were little more than personal servants. As they spoke, I had a déjà vu kind of experience. *I've heard this kind of talk before*, I thought to myself. And it dawned on me: I'd heard it in some churches. I've had the privilege of being in lots of churches, and I've overheard that kind of talk from parishioners about ministers. Those folks around that table could just as easily have been talking about the ministers at their church as about the servers at their country club. In some churches the ministerial staff are viewed in the same light as the club staff.

If you find yourself in that kind of congregation, then my counsel would be either to gently lead them to a biblical model of church or to do what you need to do, through whatever channels are available in your tradition, to find another church. You will never have the authority to lead in that church if its members see you as little more than a paid servant.

Generational Perspectives

What about our differing generational perspectives on authority?

Speaking stereotypically, strong leadership is rather suspect among younger generations. When you assert your leadership rights and responsibilities, it feels to many in their twenties and thirties like you are going Attila the Hun on them. It seems hard for some to distinguish between putting one's foot down and stepping over a line.[6]

Of course, corporate-style leadership became popular among pastors during *my* generation (I was born in 1959). It's my generation of pastors who popularized Jack Welch's leadership style. The rather flat leadership preference of Mosaics and Millennials is perhaps a mere correction for the hierarchical obsession of us Boomers.

While generational perspectives may be at work, it's also possible that this generational argument about whether leadership is top-down or flat misses the point altogether. What we really need is situational leadership—where we shape our leadership style to fit the situation. This approach actually transcends generations. No matter our age or the age of those we're leading, there are situations in which gently offering a word as a peer is appropriate. At other times we have to be out front leading the charge. And still other times we may need to provide a good ol' verbal kick-in-the-seat-of-the-pants—in Christian love, of course. Good leaders adjust their style to the situation regardless of which generation they are from or which generations they are leading.

What about a Team of Overseers?

Among some of our most admirable young churchmen, there is the idea that a team of leaders—a pastoral team—is far superior to the proverbial one-man show. It's a popular idea in many young circles.

I've confessed that it was from my generation that the "CEO-pastor" model emerged. And I acknowledge that, while good leadership is good leadership, and spiritual leaders can learn from those who lead in the corporate arena, those who revel in the executive role don't look like shepherd-leaders at all. So what do we do?

I know some wonderful young congregations whose answer to this matter is a *team* of pastors, each of whom steps forward to lead depending on the situation and his or her giftedness. Those churches certainly are not unbiblical, and they might be on to something. In fact, I'm coming around on the team approach. I see how valuable it would be in minimizing loneliness and discouragement, as well as maximizing effectiveness. Furthermore,

I believe a more flat leadership structure would give us credibility with the emerging generations. The hierarchical approach popularized by my generation, the Baby Boomers, is going to be a tough sell for my children's generation.

J. R. Woodward has argued well for *polycentric leadership*—"a shift from the traditional hierarchical approach to leadership to a communal polycentric approach...the sweet spot between centralization and decentralization."[7] The collaborative, organic, grass-roots-oriented, relational, transparent, accessible, no-one-person-has-all-the-gifts, we're-all-in-this-together model is increasingly attractive for me. In fact, if I ever were to go back to local church ministry, I believe I could enjoy living out this model.

Still, I believe the norm is one overseer for one congregation. Church history supports the one-overseer-per-congregation model. If we look at the first church, the Jerusalem church, on the surface it looks like a kind of shared leadership. I believe James, however, was the clear and primary leader. Furthermore, if we look at some of the other early churches, we do find elders functioning as leadership teams; yet clearly Paul, Timothy, and Titus were solitary figures at the helms of various congregations. Then by the second century, the single office of pastor—located in one person—was clearly the norm. So while one might argue that the original church leadership structure was unclear in regards to a solitary pastor, it certainly wasn't long until the solitary-leader role emerged.

When it comes to churches facing difficult times, whether the causes are internal or external, those are the times when having a single leader are especially important. In Leonard Sweet's book, *The Perfect Storm*, Bill Easum made a compelling case for such situations:

> The future church will require a stronger, more focused, single leader than ever before. A ship can have only one captain when it turns into a storm. Anything else is a disaster.
>
> I know a lot has been written about team-based ministry, and I'm all for it, as long as the team has a single leader. Every thriving form of life has one, single, organizing principle. The same is true for the church. The

church will need leaders who lead and who do not blink in times of chaos.[8]

Even when there is a team of leaders, one person almost always emerges as the one to whom others naturally look. I'd suggest that's simply the way God wired us. So the answer to runaway egos is not necessarily leadership by committee. The answer is collaborative overseers who remember they are also shepherds.

Oh, and while we're considering Bill Easum's observations, he has another one that fits in this discussion about spiritual oversight:

> [M]ost of the churches using forms of congregational or representative democracy are leftovers from modernity and are on life support. On the other hand, the vast majority of thriving churches today are apostolic, or pastor-led. We've also noted that the thriving churches using congregational and representative forms of governance have figured out how to circumvent as much of their governance systems as possible... Even if these pastors function in a denomination that requires democratic rule, they find ways to get around or minimize its effects and provide biblical leadership.[9]

I have long believed that a rigid congregational approach results in unnecessary quagmires and controversy for missional churches. Whether it's a new church with many young believers or an established church whose vision has resulted in real complexity, congregational government has its limitations. A congregational approach is best for small-to-mid-size churches who are content to maintain their size and effectiveness. When a church is passionate about people far from God and willing to join God in an aggressive approach to reaching them, a small circle of deeply spiritual and well-informed leaders—a mix of mature laity and clergy—can make better decisions than a room of people who cannot possibly have the entire picture. Though my tradition affirms and limits itself to the congregational model, it seems to me that an elder-like approach allows a team of spiritually mature, competent, and collaborative people to offer accountability for, and partnership with, a senior pastor in the leadership of a complex, growing congregation with a heart for mission.

Now, let's get back to the matter of team leadership vs. a solitary leader. There is no absolute right and wrong here. At the same time, I would contend that the best leadership model is a team of lay and clerical leaders with one deeply spiritual and competent person who has a humble, collegial, willing-to-share-authority spirit as the one with whom the buck stops. Yet, I'm increasingly open to a team approach, not because I believe it to be the best model of leadership, but because it is perhaps the best model of leadership for our non-hierarchical age. And while I am increasingly drawn to the team leadership model, I believe Easum is at least partially right: the waters into which we are sailing are so tumultuous that we need one strong person at the wheel—an overseer.

Abuse of Power

One day I looked up from my computer screen to a framed picture of three wolves that had sat on my desk for years. It's one of those "Successories" pictures that are supposed to motivate people in the workplace. Someone had given me this picture. One of the three wolves is standing proudly in front of the others; he's unquestionably the dominant one. The caption beneath reads "Leadership." I picked up the picture and tossed it in the trashcan. I was suddenly struck by the fact that I had been looking for years at an image of a leader as a proud wolf. The alpha wolf. I just didn't feel good about that image anymore. Not for a pastor. [10]

Why do some of us like playing the role of an alpha wolf? Could it be true that some spiritual leaders assume the domineering role when we are least confident in who we are and what we are doing? Reggie McNeal thinks so. He wrote, "Some leaders...claim to operate from 'spiritual authority' when in fact they are operating out of a deep sense of insecurity." [11] I believe a lot of overbearing leaders are acting out of their poor self-esteem and their feelings of inadequacy. If I do not feel good about myself—if I am insecure and feel inferior—then I have a constant need to prove myself, to exert my authority, and to try to convince myself and others that I am *not* inferior. I throw my weight around to cover-up for what I feel are inadequacies.

When we are comfortable with who we are, we do not have to prove our worth by positioning ourselves as someone important. If

I am not suffering from a lack of self-esteem, then I can admit that I am not always right. I can admit that others are more intelligent or more gifted than I, and I am not threatened by that. But if my confidence is a little shaky...well, then...

For four years, our family lived in Nigeria where we were missionaries. There I taught in the Nigerian Baptist Theological Seminary. Some of my Nigerian seminary students lived through a difficult but learning experience for me. Early on I was asked to teach a course that was out of my area of expertise. When the semester began, I had been out of seminary myself for only a year and a half. In that class I felt insecure, inadequate, and had little self-confidence. Because I was the young lecturer and had a newly earned PhD after my name, I felt I had to prove myself to the class. I felt I needed to hide my weaknesses lest the students find out how little I actually knew. So when difficult questions were asked, I felt threatened. When questions were raised for which I had no answers, I was insulted. I felt people in the class were intentionally trying to embarrass me. I became defensive and irritable in the class. I had been with the same group of students for another subject during the previous semester (a subject for which I was prepared and in which I felt confident), and we had enjoyed each other a great deal. But nobody was having fun this time around, and it was my fault.

One evening we met together for a makeup class. I was irritable, and I responded brusquely to some of the questions. My insecurities had caused me to be rather tyrannical. After class dismissed, a student—a brave and wise student—followed me to my office and asked for a moment to talk with me. He was not impolite or disrespectful, but he was candid. He asked, "Have we done something to offend you? You don't seem to like us very much."

I was deeply convicted by his observations. When the class met on the next day, before I began my lecture, I explained my problem and confessed my sin to the class. I asked for their understanding and forgiveness. I acknowledged that my insecurity had turned me into a dictator. The students were gracious. The next time I preached in chapel to the student body, I told my story and again confessed. I had abused my authority and jeopardized my influence. I had to come clean.

I began to learn something with that experience: the less secure I am, the harder I try to prove my worth and competence.

What I needed to embrace is the truth of the matter: We do not make ourselves people of worth by hiding our limitations or by showing off; we *are* people of worth because God formed us and loves us and has determined we are of great worth. We do not make ourselves people of value by demonstrating our competence. We *are* people of great value because God created us and loves us and has determined that we are of great value. You and I don't *create* meaning and purpose for our lives; we simply *accept* the meaning and purpose that we have purely because God decided we are of great value. We don't have to establish our worth by exercising our authority.

I have learned a great deal from the writings of the Ghanain Christian leader, Gottfried Osei-Mensah. He offered "a warning particularly to young pastors and teachers who, with the impulse and impatience of youth, may attempt to ride roughshod over the feelings and sensitivities of a congregation of God's church."[12] He added that young, insecure ministers in particular are tempted to throw their weight around, and that if they do, they will alienate many people and have a difficult time. That's true for all ministers, regardless of their age.

Never forget, my friend, that you are a miracle of God. If you will remember how highly valued *you* are by your Creator, your congregation will then appreciate how highly you value *them*.

Overseers as Prophets

One day I was talking to a man who was serving as a consultant to our church. Sitting at Starbucks I told him, "You can say things that I can't say." I was thinking of those hard things, those challenging things, those things that might upset the order and make people mad. I'd heard pastors say that about guest preachers.

"I fully understand that," he told me.

"People who blow in and blow out can say things I can't, because I have to stay around afterwards!" I complained.

The next day I was mowing my lawn and reliving the conversation of the previous day. Echoing in my mind (along with my iPod's inspiring mix of Motown, 70s rock, and contemporary country) were my words to the consultant, "You can say things

I can't say." And I thought to myself, "Really?! An outsider can say things that the pastor can't say? Is that the way it should be?"

I've concluded that, indeed, that is *not* the way things should be. One of the responsibilities of the overseer is to make prophetic, hard statements. That local overseer has earned the right to be prophetic, or at least *should* have. And the fact that he or she is going to be around afterward adds value to what is said.

It's true that the outsider often has a unique and valuable perspective, and people sometimes will hear hard things better from an outsider than from one they know well. Yet, the one who has invested his or her life in the congregation, and who will be around to help people deal with the tough issues, has both a responsibility and right to make difficult declarations.

So, my minister friend, don't shrink from the role of prophet.

Unwelcome Remarks from the Outside

What about fellow ministers in other churches who take pot shots at you?

Sometimes you will have to lead your church creatively and aggressively while enduring snide remarks from fellow members of the ministerial fraternity. If you color outside the proverbial lines, you will be derided by jealous pastors nearby who fault your methods when their methods are failing, by seminary professors who are "passionately processing their two years in the ministry fifteen years ago,"[13] and by seminary students whose untested certainty you will find frustrating. You'll hear a cry for flat leadership from progressive-thinking folks who believe the pastor should sit with church members and hum and let the vision arise by magical consensus. Your church's creative worship style will be the object of scorn from ministers who worship tradition. Sometimes you will have to lead despite unfair criticism from really smart (if naïve) people.

In many circles there is a definite prejudice against strong leadership. There are some who dismiss this idea as a right-wing abuse of power. But spiritual oversight is not the invention of power-hungry fundamentalists. It's God's idea.

Frankly, many congregations led by enlightened pastors who decry authoritarianism and champion the equal sharing of leadership are dying. They have overreacted to the pastors/

dictators and have let the pendulum swing too far in the other direction. Remember Bill Self's words: "More churches are hurt by pastoral default than have ever been hurt by pastoral domination."

Have you ever heard of the "crabs in a barrel" mentality? I know little about crabs, but apparently when a crab looks like he is climbing out above the others, the rest of the crabs will grab with their claws and pull that rising crab back down to their level. Don't let crabs...er...champions of egalitarianism...dampen your commitment to oversight.

Should You Declare Your Authority?

So should your next step be to declare your authority?

While working on this chapter, I came across Joe McKeever's "100 Tips for Leaders That Everyone in Ministry Should Know." Here is tip #4: "Your church members should submit to your leadership, but you're not the one to tell them that."[14]

I knew a pastor who often preached on the authority of the pastor. "Touch not my anointed" (1 Chron. 16:22) was one of his common themes. He loved to tell the story of those juvenile wisenheimers who dared disrespect Elisha. You might remember that they were the ones eaten by the infamous she-bears.

Please don't be that pastor who loves to threaten his or her people with God's judgment if they don't go along with you. Remember that spiritual authority is mainly that of influence, not mandates. Let your spiritual authority speak for itself.

If All Else Fails

If, after all this, you feel your church is suffering because of a misunderstanding of the biblical model of church leadership, here are some suggestions:

1. Check your motives.

Pride is as hard to detect in our hearts as carbon monoxide is in our houses. And as deadly. J. Oswald Sanders advised: "When a person rises in position, as happens to leaders in the church, the tendency to pride also increases. If not checked, the attitude will disqualify the person from further advancement in the kingdom of God, for 'the Lord detests the proud of heart' (Proverbs 16:5)."[15]

This conversation about oversight can never, ever, be about *us*. Not about our ego needs. Not about our insecurities. Not about our shallow desire to impress our increasingly successful friends. Certainly not about pushing our churches beyond reasonable limits to reach goals that will make *us* feel important. This conversation absolutely has to be about what God had in mind when He spoke through Paul about the role of pastors.

2. Know that heavy-handedness almost always backfires.

George Bullard wrote a helpful article titled "What If It Really Is the Pastor's Fault?"[16] There he told the story of a congregation who voted down a seemingly wonderful proposal to sponsor and house a much-needed Korean congregation. The reasons stated in opposition to the proposal were absurd, and the pastor was disheartened. But what if, Bullard asked, it indeed was the pastor's fault that the congregation had made this decision? You'll have to read the article to get the full story, but in essence the pastor's problem was that he was "a strong-willed pastor fully equipped with blinders." The vote to reject the Korean congregation, Bullard suggests, was more a referendum on his leadership than a repudiation of the Korean group.

The point is, sometimes even a great vision can be jeopardized by overassertive leadership.

3. Know that trust is earned and that usually takes time.

If your congregation has had a history of skilled staff ministers who have established trust in ministerial leadership, then build on that and don't blow it. But if in your church's history ministers have made some boneheaded decisions, then it will take years for you to earn the right to determine the course your church will take. Be patient.

If you'll recall, Joe McKeever's #4 tip was, "Your church members should submit to your leadership, but you're not the one to tell them that." Well, here is McKeever's tip #5: "The best way to get people to submit to your leadership is for you to humble yourself and serve them the way the Lord did the disciples (John 13); they will trust someone who loves them that much."[17]

4. Recognize the weaknesses and shortcomings of staff ministers.

In certain areas, you will need to call on financial experts, human resource specialists, counselors, engineers, project managers, and a bunch of other folks who are likely to be better skilled (at least in certain areas) than you or your staff ministers are. The ability to recognize where others are more skilled is critical. A problem in some churches is that sometimes church staff members make decisions without adequate research or even for which we are not qualified. When we do that, we risk losing people's trust. A few significant missteps and it will be a long time before folks give us more than a short rope.

After you've completed suggestions 1 through 4…

5. Raise the governance question.

We had good conversations in my previous church about this topic, and a blue-ribbon study team was enlisted to tackle our church governance. It was a terribly involved process, and they were still at work when I left for my present ministry. They were asking: "What can ministers approve and what does the congregation need to approve? Are ministers striking the balance between overseeing and shepherding? Are we appropriately acknowledging the priesthood of the believers? What does 'oversight' mean in our place? Are spiritual leaders given the authority commensurate with their responsibility?" The conversation is ongoing, but I'm certain they are going to end up at a good place for that congregation.

I was blessed to be part of a church that allowed me to raise the issue without hauling me over the coals. If you are respectful and patient, and if your ego needs are not the motivation, you might be surprised at how willing church members are to talk about the matter.

6. Clarify the parameters.

Figure out how big the sandbox is that you've been given to play in. Daniel Sherman said it this way: "You might have more control than you think you do. Try to test the limits. See if your limited control is only your perception. Make a decision on your own. Invite a guest speaker without asking. Do something that stretches the boundaries a bit and see if you get in trouble. You might be freer than you think you are!"[18]

7. Gently educate people.

I offer this suggestion with some trepidation, for my suggestion that you "gently educate people" might be twisted by some to mean "Set the people straight!" I'm not talking about setting people straight, but I know a lot of ministers are on power trips and that is exactly what they're doing.

Here's my point. As you "declare the whole counsel of God," don't be afraid to teach the texts that deal with spiritual leadership. You certainly may, and should, teach and preach those texts as you walk through Scripture with God's people. Don't, however, arrogantly (and foolishly) talk too much about your authority.

Be diplomatic and subtle, not blatant and obnoxious. Look for particular opportunities to bring young influencers along. Remember, the goal is to gently educate people. As you mentor young leaders, speak about the leadership dance between ministers and laity. Talk about the texts I'm covering in this chapter, and help people understand what the Bible says about spiritual oversight.

8. Work within your church's polity until and unless the church's polity changes.

Your role will be determined largely by your congregation's polity. Those pastors whose churches have elders will lead their elders and lead the church through their elders. Those who have bishops over them lead under the authority of bishops. Those who serve churches with congregational church government will lead by influence and persuasion of the membership, not by decree. Within each category there are numerous variations, depending on the individual church's culture. So understand the ground rules by which you're playing.

Multiple years and increasing trust may enable you to lead effectively no matter how constricting you feel your church's governance is. And, over time, you might even affect a power shift.

What you don't want to do is walk into a church and blatantly defy their polity or culture. I've seen arrogant new pastors immediately assume more power than people are accustomed to granting. That kind of reckless wrenching of the reins from the congregation rarely ends well.

9. Remember, can isn't necessarily should.

First Corinthians 10:23 tells us that an action's permissibility does not guarantee its profitability. That's a good reminder for spiritual leaders. The fact that we could garner the votes for something and justify it under the banner of spiritual authority doesn't mean we should do it. Such values as honoring people and treating others as we'd like to be treated remind us that the fact that we *can* doesn't mean we *should*.

10. Be careful what you ask for.

I suggest that you pause before asking for more oversight. To whom much is given, much is expected. And if you ask for more responsibility, you might just get it. Then the pressure will be much more intense. The decisions you make will be scrutinized, your calls will be questioned, and your reputation will be on the line. It shouldn't be any other way. That kind of pressure, however, is considerable.

Spiritual Authority Is Yours

Because some parishioners are mature, they will want you to exercise it.

Because some of them are suspicious, they will not acknowledge it.

Because some are lazy, they will blindly and unquestioningly surrender to it.

You and just about everybody else will struggle to define it.

But one thing is for sure: You've got it, my friend. God gave you spiritual authority when He called you to be a vocational minister. You have oversight of His church.

Now, before you call a meeting of your leaders and tell them you're in charge from now on...before you declare yourself sovereign...before you preach that sermon about the guys who snubbed Elisha and got eaten by the she-bears...let's talk about shepherding.

7

Shepherds vs. Hired Hands

"Shepherd the Church of God..."

He said, "Lord, you know all things; you know
that I love you."
Jesus said, "Feed my sheep."

—JOHN 21:17B

I believe God inspired Paul to immediately follow his words about "overseeing" with these words about "shepherding": "Be shepherds of the church of God" (Acts 20:28). This shepherd-talk is a good balance to the talk about being the overseers of congregations. But shepherding isn't easy.

Jon McIntosh said that he took an informal poll of his minister friends and asked them, "What recently has made you want to quit?" The #3 response was, "The Hard Work of Shepherding." Furthermore, a church planter responded that he was unpleasantly surprised that after the church is planted, he has to actually pastor people! The church planter added: "Coming to the reality that we can't just make cool Web sites, network in the community, and launch a church. We actually have to do the hard work of shepherding."[1]

What you do is hard. And one reason why is the hard work of shepherding. Being a minister would be easier for most of us if we could sit in our offices and issue edicts or just read stuff.

Pastor John Ames, a pastor in the novel *Gilead*, described the pure joy that came from entering his church's old sanctuary early in the morning, watching the dawn awaken through its windows, and hearing the sacred creaks of its floor. Then he confessed, "After a while I did begin to wonder if I liked the church better with no people in it."[2]

Yet there is no church without people in it. And God never envisioned an ivory tower ministry for His people. One of the best reminders of that is the book *They Smell Like Sheep,* by Lynn Anderson. Years ago Anderson wrote his book in response to the growing body of literature produced by church leaders that was borrowing from the secular, corporate world. Anderson reacted negatively to the "CEO/Chairman of the Board" model. He lamented that some pastors "regard fellowship events, small groups, and in-depth personal discussions as 'fluff' or 'touchy-feely' stuff—which, like quiche, is not palatable to 'real men.'"[3] Anderson reminded us that the very word "pastor" gives us our job description; we are first and foremost shepherds!

To shepherd is to protect and care for the flock—to tend to their wounds and their brokenness. To shepherd a congregation is to help carry their burdens and to seek them when they wander. To shepherd people is to feed them, making sure they have what they need for spiritual growth, cheering for them without coddling them. It is also to walk in front of, to humbly yet boldly show the way for, the Church of God. It is no small thing to be a spiritual shepherd.

A Confession

Here's a confession. As a local church pastor, sometimes I liked the "overseer" part better than the "shepherd" part. Truth is, I liked feeling a little bit like an executive. I have friends who are professionals in non-ministry vocations, and I liked talking with them about leadership issues. About change theory. About budgeting in uncertain economic times. About Patrick Lencioni, Jim Collins, and Peter Drucker. I didn't particularly like talking about shepherding, particularly with my football official buddies. It sounded a little wimpy. Kind of soft. Shepherding the flock often seems like the job of someone with a soft voice who likes "heartwarming" movies. It's much more impressive to talk about oversight.

But then someone from the church would say, "I'd like you to meet my pastor," or, "I'm so glad you're my pastor," or one of the kids would call me "Pastor Travis." And that felt so right. I'll admit it; it was *heartwarming*. Down deep, "This is my pastor," felt much better than, "This is my overseer." Now that I am not the pastor of a local church, it is the role of shepherd that I miss most.

I look back now and see so many ways I could have shepherded better. I have faces in my memory of those who wandered from the flock when I was too wrapped up with the ninety-nine to tend to the one. I remember those whose wounds bled while I tended to the machinery of the church. Others have done so much better than I did at this. Yet I did love being the shepherd.

Understanding Shepherds

To understand our shepherd role, we need to have the right image of a shepherd in mind. Most of us probably picture a shepherd as someone with a placid smile carrying a lamb lovingly in his arms—a gentle soul with a soothing voice and nonthreatening demeanor. You know, *soft*. Perhaps we have confused love for sheep with a fondness for teddy bears.

Real shepherds aren't saps. They fight off predators, risk their lives to rescue lost sheep, and have skin like leather. Sissies don't shepherd sheep. Bill Hull is very helpful here:

> The Hebrew *roeh* and the Greek *poimen* have common meanings. *Roeh* means "to feed, to keep, to lead."… The contextual usage in both testaments refers to the leadership of God's people… Note that God considered prophets, priests and kings shepherds. Kings of Assyria and Babylon were to shepherd the people, to protect and provide. The condemnation of "the shepherds of Israel" in Ezekiel 34 was directed against rulers… If we are to understand shepherding we must rid ourselves of the modern portrayal of shepherds as passive, weak, and unable to lead in the real world of politics, business, and world affairs… Old Testament usage defines shepherding as "leading a people." This includes all of life: commerce, education, foreign affairs, and providing the proper environment and instruction for spiritual life.[4]

That is the biblical portrait of a shepherd. Hull believes, as I do, that the terms "elders, bishop and pastor" are used synonymously and that the function of a biblical shepherd is two-fold: oversight and care.

The Concierge-Chaplain?

Being a shepherd is not about being the concierge-chaplain. You are a servant to all; a concierge to no one. A concierge serves customers and guests. A concierge sees to it that people are content and comfortable. He or she asks, "How may I make your stay here more delightful?"

You, however, are not a concierge. It's one thing to love people so much we look not to our own interests but to the interests of others (see Phil. 2:4). It's quite another to have as one's priority making everybody happy.

It's one thing to have a servant's heart. It's quite another to prostitute ourselves. And, yes, I used "prostitute" intentionally. Many of us minister-types do things we don't really like for the "payment" of affirmation. Many of us will do anything, including violate our convictions, to hear someone say "Good job." Few of us are in this for the money. More than a few of us, however, live for approval. Don't forget the words of Paul: "Am I now trying to win the approval of human beings, or of God? Or am I trying to please people? If I were still trying to please people, I would not be a servant of Christ" (Gal. 1:10).

So let's remember: we're shepherds, not concierge-ministers.

Can "Shepherd" Be a Cop-Out?

Let's admit that sometimes the title "shepherd" can be a cop-out for us. Many pastors who emphasize their roles as shepherds are abdicating their roles as prophets and leaders. A lot of us justify our lack of leadership and our churches' lack of growth by claiming the role of shepherd. We rationalize away the fact that no one's life has been genuinely transformed in a long time by the flimsy claim that we were called just to "love the people."

In the book *Quiet Conversations*, the fictitious church researcher David says:

> The phrase, "I was called to be the shepherd of my flock" is always the trump card stated by pastors in stagnant or dying congregations. By the way, we never hear that kind of imagery from pastors of thriving congregations… [P]astors of congregations effectively reaching unchurched people never use the shepherd metaphor. They describe their work in terms used by missionaries.[5]

So which comes first—the chicken or the egg? Do congregations stagnate because pastors see themselves first as chaplains and caregivers, or do pastors resign themselves to the role of chaplains and caregivers because they see their churches declining? Or do declining churches and shepherds/chaplains/caregivers simply attract each other? I don't know, but let's not use the title "shepherd" as an excuse to shrink from assertive and outwardly focused leadership. "I'm a shepherd" can be a cop-out, a rationalization for tepid, timid, timorous behavior.

So, on the one hand, mamby-pamby leadership in the name of shepherding is not leadership at all. On the other hand, overly aggressive, personal-agenda-driven, "people are getting in the way of my plan" leadership is narcissistic grandstanding.

A Balanced Perspective

Here is a balanced way to look at shepherding God's people. It comes from one of my good friends, Tim Clark. Tim used to raise sheep. He has been a vocational minister for more than three decades now; the sheep were a hobby. But he learned a lot about Christian leadership from that wooly avocation. Tim once wrote:

> One day I got a call from our neighbor telling me that our sheep had gotten out of the fencing and were in her yard... eating her flowers! I hung up the phone and started for the door when I ran into a fellow minister who was extremely athletic and I asked him if he could come and help me get my sheep back in the fencing. When we got to the farm my friend jumped out of the truck and started running in a panic for the sheep. He ran after them, chasing them, and the harder he ran the more the sheep scattered. Picture a grown man running as fast as he could across a rough 20 acre field trying to chase the sheep into submission and back to the barn. Now my flock of sheep was scattered to every corner of the rather large field. I walked down the lane, next to the large field with the widely scattered sheep and shook a bucket with a small amount of corn and called for the sheep the way I had called them all of their lives. They heard that sound, looked at me and came running. I led them ... walked in front of them...leading them back to the barn and they came together in a tight flock and

followed. Cattle are herded…get behind them and yell and they move and come together. Sheep have to be led…from the front. "He 'leadeth' me beside still waters!"[6]

Shepherds are not cowboys, but they are leaders nonetheless. They need to lead in ways their flock will understand and follow. First Peter 5:1–3 speaks of our role in caring for people entrusted to us:

> To the elders among you, I appeal as a fellow elder and a witness of Christ's sufferings who also will share in the glory to be revealed: Be shepherds of God's flock that is under your care, watching over them—not because you must, but because you are willing, as God wants you to be; not pursuing dishonest gain, but eager to serve; not lording it over those entrusted to you, but being examples to the flock.

Being an overseer means assuming God-given authority. But being a shepherd means not being intoxicated by, or abusive with, that authority. Being a mature Christ-follower involves recognizing the calling and responsibilities of the spiritual leader (Heb. 13:17). But this does not entail the conferral of carte-blanche power to the leader or the exercise of blind loyalty for the followers. A balance needs to be achieved.

Church Growth and Shepherding

A factor that impacts a minister's shepherding role is church growth. As the church grows, shepherding takes on a different look. Growth changes ministers' attention to increasingly focus on new members, preparation for preaching and teaching, casting the vision, and overseeing new ministries. All those things draw ministers away from one on one caregiving. Nevertheless, the leader of a growing church can still be a shepherd. He or she can still make sure that the congregation's pastoral needs are met.

To accomplish this, I would suggest not becoming isolated from the needs of the congregation, even if that congregation is growing larger and more complex. For example, I believe even the senior pastor of a large church should be part of a rotation for hospital visitation. You can delegate that, but I fear you will forfeit some relational capital. Furthermore, even if you don't have the time or the skills to be a counselor, doing your best to meet with members of your church family who request a conversation is important if you are going to shepherd effectively. If your conversation demonstrates they need more help than you can provide you can, and should, refer them to professionals you know and trust. There might even be other ministers on staff who are gifted counselors who could provide more intensive, long-term care that would be helpful.

A church's numerical growth and increasing complexity will result in its ministers seeming ever more inaccessible and unapproachable. I don't see any way to counter that. You can, however, build into your schedule those meaningful appearances at events celebrated by various groups in the congregation and other expressions of genuine concern for them.

If church members feel their ministers care, and that they are being cared for, they are more likely to embrace the growth and aggressive vision of the church. If they feel neglected they might resent, or even undermine, the growth that is behind their neglect. Yet, balance is tough, and anyone who tries to be a sheepherder for hundreds of people will be pulled and tugged to the point of burnout. So what else is the shepherd of a larger church or growing church to do?

One answer is that offered by the late Calvin Miller, but I don't like his answer. I love Calvin Miller and his body of work; he was a great man and a super writer. I've quoted him in this book. But I think he missed the point on this one. Here is his suggestion: "Never have more members than you can know personally."[7] Then Miller quoted Richard Baxter: "We must labor to be acquainted, not only with the persons, but with the state of all people, with their inclinations and conversations... Doth not a careful shepherd look after every individual sheep?"[8] While a warm sentiment, the notion is simply impractical in many situations. Baxter's counsel certainly has merit for long tenures that give us opportunities to get to know the people we serve and lead. And his counsel can be wonderfully effective in small congregations. (In fact, I believe small congregations are going to be very attractive in the future.) Nevertheless, if God grows our congregation so that it gets too big for us to remember everyone's name, are we to tell new folks not to come? Oh, we could start a new church. But is that what God wants in every case? Are large churches somehow less than God's intent? Of course not. There is an important place in God's

Kingdom for large churches. And we cannot expect the pastor of a large church to serve with the same level of intimacy and familiarity that we could expect from a small church minister. That's not rocket science. But actually remembering that's the case and explaining those differing expectations to a congregation can be wonderfully clarifying and liberating for the shepherd of a large flock.

What Congregations Are Not

The image of the shepherd reminds us that the congregation is not a project and the members aren't the enemy. Eugene Peterson, in *Under the Unpredictable Plant*, says: "The congregation is not the enemy. Pastoral work is not adversarial."[9]

What prompted Peterson to write these words? I think I know. I think it's because some ministers are swaggering bullies. I've seen ministers brag about how many congregational rivals they've run off. Some megalomaniacal ministers think it's cool to be cold.

The fact that a church doesn't fit our vision of the perfect church doesn't mean it needs fixing by us; and the fact that church members simply disagree with us doesn't mean we're called by God to put them in their place or chase them out.

Shepherds and Hired Hands

There are two kinds of folks who watch sheep—real shepherds and hired hands. Hired hands don't care about the sheep as much. They are doing the job for what they can get out of it, not because they are putting the welfare of the sheep above their own. Jesus anticipated that some of his under-shepherds would use their sheep for egocentric purposes, acting more like hired hands. He even suggested they aren't true shepherds (John 10).

A real shepherd is not a hired hand. A real shepherd owns the sheep and loves them. A hired hand is looking for a way to earn a living or earn some extra money; he agrees to watch the sheep for pay. A hired hand will make sure the sheep eat. He will count the sheep. He will keep them together. But if push comes to shove—e.g., a predator attacks the sheep—he is likely to scram. Those aren't *his* sheep, after all; they're just a way to make a few shekels.

Jesus' teaching about the sheep and the hired hands is told in the context of the mistreatment of people by their religious leaders.

The so-called spiritual guides of Jesus' day used their positions for personal gain. They enjoyed the power, prestige, and privilege of their position and loved to flaunt it. In short, the religious leaders were acting like hired hands. They didn't really love the people; they *used* the people.

Perhaps the adversarial relationships between vocational ministers and the people they serve is often a result of hired hands leading churches. Of course, many vocational ministers have laughingly said, "Being a minister would be great if it weren't for the people!" But if there is truth behind that for us, then we might have either missed our calling or become ineffectively calloused. Shepherds see people as the point of their ministry, not an obstacle to their ministry.

The following are some of the characteristics of a spiritual shepherd.

A Real Shepherd Is Patient with People

A person who is interested in fulfilling his or her personal goals and enriching his or her resume will expect everyone to move at his or her pace, to fulfill his or her goals, to give more than they are able to give. A real shepherd, however, is patient with people.

If you are always charging ahead, make sure you don't get so far ahead that people give up on you. Perhaps you will be disappointed with what appears to be an apathetic response to your call for action. In your more cynical moments, you might wonder if the people are asleep, lazy, or coldhearted. At that point you have two options. You can throw up your hands and cry, like Elijah under the juniper tree, "I am the only one left on earth who wants to serve God!" (1 Kings 19). Or, you can be patient. I would encourage you to take the second option: be patient. Don't give up on the vision; just give people a little time to catch up with you. After all, you are thinking about this matter night and day, and the vision might have been in your heart and head for months. Slow down long enough for the good people behind you to digest the idea.

One of the most helpful resources I've found is William J. Webb's book *Women, Slaves and Homosexuality*. Webb writes about what he calls the "redemptive-movement hermeneutic." It's a way of interpreting the Bible by intentionally noticing its movement, its progression on important issues. My simple summary of Webb's insights is this: God took the people of the Bible where they were, and then He "nudged" His people toward life as it should be lived, knowing He couldn't jerk them immediately into a mature Judeo-Christian ethic. Here's the way Webb put it: "Sometimes God's instructions are simply designed to get his flock moving... As one of my mentors used to say to me, 'You don't back the truck up and dump it all at once!'"[10]

What God said about important social and spiritual matters was often in stark contrast to the messages His people were getting from their culture. So God took them at their level of understanding and led them like a shepherd in the right direction. That provides a good example for us to follow.

Likewise, "under-shepherds" understand that they have neither the right nor the clout to force, jerk, or otherwise rush people into decisions. When we do that, at best people tend to offer verbal assent and hide their true opinions under the cloak of conformity. Shepherds don't inflict their impatience upon their congregation.

Shepherds Get out of the Office

Some of us don't like "administrivia," but we still have to do it. Others of us use administrative responsibilities as an excuse not to get involved with people. For some of us, studying a little bit more, or working on the weekly newsletter a little bit more, or tweaking the website, or...name it...is easier than going to a nursing home, visiting the children's hospital, or dropping by the office of a staff member whose family is struggling.

We cannot allow ourselves to choose office work over people work. I can't say I did a great job at this. Many who read this will have done a far better job than I did at getting out of the office. But the bottom line is that attention to people is more important than attention to office details.

We also have to be careful not to let the machinery of the church steal our time and energy. There are so many programs to run. So many committee meetings to attend. So many e-mails to return. The machine will eat you up. And no one can remedy that except you.

I never quite succeeded at building a church infrastructure that gave me time for just hanging out with people. Yet I encourage you to make sure the congregational systems—from governance to staffing—allow you the time and energy to go, at least now and then, to the senior adult luncheons and on the youth mission trips.

Shepherds Really "Behold" People

Mark 10:21 reads, "Then Jesus beholding him loved him" (KJV). In her book on leadership, *Jesus CEO*, Laurie Beth Jones quoted that verse and wrote about how important it is to *behold* people. To "behold" someone is to *be* fully centered on that person and to *hold* that person in your heart and mind during that significant moment.[11] Have you ever been talking with someone and felt that, in those moments, you were the most important person in the world to him or her? That's "beholding." On the other hand, have you ever been talking to someone who seemed to be constantly glancing around the room to see who else was there? That's *not* "beholding."

When we are speaking with someone, instead of thinking up our next lines or looking around the room to see who else might be there, let's "behold" the person. One of the greatest gifts you can give to a person is your presence, your undivided attention. Let's listen to people. When they are sitting in our offices, let's listen instead of spending so much energy trying to come up with wise answers. And when we're standing in the worship centers, let's really listen to people instead of looking over their shoulders for the influencers. Let's listen to people on the phone and read the serious e-mails carefully. Let's know the names and the stories of the members of the custodial staff.

Jesus served people by beholding them. Shepherds do that.

Shepherds Put People Ahead of Schedules and Projects

Some of Jesus' best ministry was a result of interruptions. An unexpected touch of his robe here; a surprise cot through the roof there. An unexpected "Help my unbelief!" here; a surprise "Heal my daughter" there. He was the quintessential man on a mission, but people were always more important than his schedule or his projects.

While Jesus served others, he did not allow them to set his agenda. He was available but not manipulatable. He knew the difference between trying to meet people's needs (which is servanthood) and trying to meet people's expectations (which is servitude). He understood boundaries. At the same time, he was not so obsessed with his schedule and projects that he was closed to the ministry of interruptions.

We must not live our lives based on other people's expectations, or allow others to set our agendas. And we need to carve out times when we are not interrupted. (I always tried to keep my mornings free for study.) Yet we can't be so obsessed with our schedules and projects that we are not open to the ministry of interruptions.

Henri Nouwen told of visiting the University of Notre Dame, where he met an older, experienced professor who had spent his teaching career in that school. As they meandered across the historic campus, the older professor reflected, "You know, my whole life I have been complaining that my work was constantly interrupted, until I discovered that my interruptions were my work."[12]

Some of our most Christlike service in the church might just be our responses to those interruptions.

Shepherds Don't Badmouth Their Sheep

The fact that being a vocational minister is hard means that you are going to struggle with your feelings toward some people—mainly people inside the churches you serve. But here is something you just have to remember: Shepherds don't badmouth their sheep. In the classic book *Life Together,* Dietrich Bonhoeffer wrote:

> A pastor should not complain about his congregation, certainly never to other people, but also not to God. A congregation has not been entrusted to him in order that he should become its accuser before God and men… Let him pray God for an understanding of his own failure, and his particular sin, and pray that he may not wrong his brethren. Let him, in the consciousness of his own guilt, make intercession for his brethren.[13]

I was tempted to leave this point out. After all, what else would pastors talk about when we get together if not our congregations? It's true, though: Shepherds (good ones) don't badmouth their sheep.

Now, let me offer a little caveat. If you need to unload, vent, or seek counsel as a shepherd leader, then you should not feel bad about telling the truth about your congregation. If a need for personal pastoral care is behind the unloading of information, so be it. But let's do that in the right, confidential, professional circles.

If we are going around badmouthing, belittling, bemoaning, and bewailing our sheep, then it's time to confess our sin and ask God for a fresh perspective. If we see our flock as adversaries, then we need either a change of heart or a change of assignments (and I suggest starting with the heart). Let's be careful not to wrong our brothers and sisters by attacking them in their absence.

Furthermore, let our prophetic pronouncements be informed by compassion. As a spiritual leader, there will be times when your convictions, observations, and insights will require corrective confrontation. Yet, as Will Willimon quoted Reinhold Neibuhr, "It is hard to speak unpleasant things to people whom one has learned to love."[14] One test of our shepherdness is whether behind our hard words there is a vindictive spirit or a heavy heart.

People grow to be spiritually mature when the truth is spoken in love (Eph. 4:15). No one benefits from either placation or flagellation.

Shepherds Protect the Flock, Even From Internal Attacks

"Guard what has been entrusted to your care" (1 Tim. 6:20a).

One role of shepherds is to protect innocent sheep from malicious sheep. If you are unwilling to confront intimidating-but-divisive people, then you need some lessons in conflict management and a good dose of nerve. An unwillingness to confront those who are hurting the church usually is a sign that our concern for our own well-being is greater than our concern for the health of the congregation. And that sounds like the hired hands Jesus talked about.

Of course, handling volunteers (i.e., church members) is different from handling employees. Yet there does come a point at which the shepherd of a congregation has to be candid even with unpaid sheep. That takes tact and guts and a ruthless examination of one's own motives. But when the flock's well-being is threatened, a good shepherd swallows hard, takes a deep breath, and says to the disruptive member, "Can we talk?"

Commentators on Acts 20 note the "between the lines" message from Paul: The trouble would not always come from outside, as they might expect; it would sometimes come from within. First

Timothy 6:4 tells us that there are some folks in the church who have an "unhealthy interest in controversies and quarrels." Some folks, Paul writes, have an unwholesome, perverted attraction to being in the middle of a fight.

Your church's mission is too important to let it be thwarted by disruptive people. As guardians of that mission, sometimes we have to confront scary people. There are times when letting the body handle a disruptive member is the right thing to do. Peer pressure can be significant, even for adults. But spiritual leadership at times requires that which so many minister-types find so repulsive: a "crucial conversation."[15]

Confrontation with difficult people should be private, at least at first; no one should be belittled before others. And remember— these difficult people are also members of the flock and you are their shepherd. However, if we are unwilling to confront disruptive sheep for the sake of the larger flock, we need to turn in our shepherd card.

Shepherds Herd the Sheep toward One Direction

Many of our churches are collections of constituencies, sometimes even competing constituencies. When that is the case, the pastor feels more like a traffic cop than a leader. We spend our time trying to make sure that everybody has a voice, isn't upset, feels included, and so on. But that's not leadership. That's indulging.

We've got to try to unite the various constituencies of our church around a common mission—a clear and compelling vision. That takes work and time. I was still trying to figure this out when I began my new ministry beyond the local church.

Shortcuts are tempting. It seems easier to plow around the proverbial stumps than to take the time to listen, and to let even antagonists help chart the church's course. On the one hand, it's not good for any organization if the one at the helm is spending an inordinate amount of time cajoling the critics; nothing ever will get accomplished. On the other hand, pushing one's agenda through without adequate communication from the leader, and without buy-in from the congregation, might look good in the short run, but it looks poor in the long run.

It's a dance. Those who fail to sound a clear call often get nothing done. Yet those who hammer the square peg until, doggone it, it fits into that round hole, find themselves with a splintered peg. You'll have to figure out your own congregation, for they're all different. You'll have to figure out when to push, when to pull, and when to back off.

In the end, you probably won't get it exactly right. Some will probably charge that you railroaded your agendas through, and others will claim you were too tenuous. And maybe they'll both be right. Remember, it's a dance.

Shepherds Are Vulnerable Leaders

Here's one of the hard things about being a shepherd: shepherds get hurt. In the words of Tom Blackaby, "As one brother in Christ once said to me, 'Sheep can bite.'"[16] In a similar vein, Kathleen S. Smith wrote, "Leaders who are out of touch with their congregations can't be hurt by them, but those who love the flock, despite its foibles, are bound to be hurt by it."[17]

I like it when people like me, and I like it even better when people are getting along. I became increasingly aware, however, that my personal popularity and peace within the congregation were not ultimate goals.

Shepherds' hearts hurt. People will say asinine, insensitive, offensive things to you, and they'll do that just because they can. Some will say rude things to you because they can't say them to their bosses at work and they just need to get the poison out of their system. Others will say nasty things to you because they are nasty people who say nasty things to lots of folks. And you'll have to take it. Much of it, anyway. You'll have to respond kindly to painfully insensitive statements. You'll have to keep your poise when most would forgive you for decking your detractor. People know the message of 1 Timothy 3, even if they can't quote it: "The overseer is to be…temperate…respectable, hospitable… gentle, not quarrelsome." So they will take advantage of that. And you'll have to bite your lip and take it.

I don't mean that you should let people abuse you. There is a line, known perhaps only by you and God, that when people cross you have to speak up. And you don't have to stay there and let your health or that of your family suffer because people don't understand propriety.

Yet, by and large, you will have to suffer insults and injuries in order to shepherd unruly sheep. People into whom you pour yourself will leave for a more "happening" church. People will say your sermons aren't expository enough or engaging enough or are not "feeding" people enough. People will question your judgment and your motives. Your car will be either too new or too old, your spouse either too involved or not involved enough. You will struggle not to become jaded and deflated.

What will keep you in the game is a shepherd's heart. And shepherd's hearts can be hurt.

It's Not Just about Spiritual Gifts

Paul's exhortation to "do the work of an evangelist" (2 Tim. 4:5) is not about having the spiritual gift of evangelism; it's about doing the work whether one has the gift or not. The same is true of shepherding. Some of us have the spiritual gifts of mercy, service, and, yes, shepherding; others of us do not. Yet all of us who bear the title "pastor," whether it's senior pastor, youth pastor, discipleship pastor, or some other kind of pastor, have the calling and responsibility to shepherd people. That means going to the hospital, the funeral home, or for an important visit in someone's living room when you'd rather be reading an article about the latest and hippest trend in ministry. And it sometimes means caring for people you don't really care for.

Meaningful Memories

Although "mercy" doesn't show up on my spiritual gifts inventory no matter how many times I take the test or which version of the test I take…although shepherding is risky and got me up close and personal both with people who love me and with those who don't care for me…although shepherding required rather mundane work when people like me would often prefer strategizing for some sort of outreach ministry…some of my most meaningful memories of the pastorate include shepherding moments: Those profound experiences in homes following a crisis. Those moving conversations in funeral homes. Written notes expressing sincere gratitude for a word or touch that I barely remember but that people said were life-changing.

Maybe one reason those shepherding moments are so satisfying is that, at least for me, it was in those moments that I was the most altruistic. I have to admit that a new outreach ministry or growth strategy always gave me a rush. But because

I'm more apostolic than compassionate in make-up, it was when I was helping heal a hurt that I was at my most selfless. Perhaps it's because I had the least to gain personally from shepherding that God blessed me with such a deep sense of satisfaction when I assumed the role of shepherd.

I believe that some timid ministers have used the title of "shepherd" as an excuse for weak leadership and to merely hold hands, singing Kumbaya, instead of trying to engage people far from God. On the other hand, I believe some of us more missional-types have dismissed the importance of being truly present in the meaningful moments of the sheep to which God has entrusted us. That is one reason why I believe God inspired Paul to combine oversight with shepherding. We all need the balance.

The Shepherd of Shepherds

There is a Shepherd whose love is so pure He would lay down his life for the sheep.

The good shepherd shows his love for the sheep in a number of ways. He rubs salve on their wounds. He leads the sheep to still waters where they can drink without fear. The good shepherd shows his love by picking the thorns and burrs out of their wool. He shows his love by extracting his sheep from the entanglement of the bushes.

But nothing matches the willingness of the shepherd to lay down his life for his sheep. The sheep's greatest threat is the predator, and nothing matches the willingness of a shepherd to stand between the blood-thirsty wolf or cougar and the defenseless herd. Nothing matches the kind of love that allows the predator to feed on the shepherd's own blood and flesh instead of that of the sheep.

The Shepherd of shepherds, Jesus, shows his love for us in many ways, like that scene in which Jesus invited the children to himself. And the shortest verse of the Bible—"Jesus wept" KJV)—comes from the story of the death of Lazarus. When Jesus saw the grief of Martha and Mary, Lazarus's sisters, he wept with them.

Jesus does care for us, and he has demonstrated that in many ways. But nothing demonstrates his love for us like that Friday when he took upon himself our sins and died.

Jesus, the Good Shepherd, is the shepherd worth following—and emulating.

8

The Church of God

"...Church of God which He bought with his blood."

The church's one foundation is Jesus Christ her Lord;
she is his new creation by water and the Word.
From heaven he came and sought her to be his holy bride;
with his own blood he bought her, and for her life he died.

—"The Church's One Foundation," Samuel J. Stone

In 1969 a little girl was growing up on Long Island, N.Y. On a Sunday morning this nine-year-old stood up to a mother whose craving for drugs was poisoning the entire family. The mother was smoking pot with her six-year-old son, and the nine-year-old big sister confronted her mom. "You can do this with your boyfriends and my older brothers," the little girl declared, "but not with my little brother."

Her mother smacked the little girl across the face. "You don't tell me what to do in my house," the doped-up mom decreed.

The nine-year-old got dressed and started walking. She ended up on the railroad tracks, and a long walk down the tracks later she happened upon an African American Pentecostal church, the doors of which were open. The little girl walked in to the sounds of the youth choir singing and sat down on the back pew.

Soon the pastor stood and preached...and preached. At a quarter to three, the pastor gave an invitation for people to come forward and accept Jesus. That little girl responded to a stirring

123

deep down inside her. She walked down the aisle with tears in her eyes and hope in her heart.

The church took her under their wing. They loved her and mentored her. When she took wrong turns, they chastised her; when she made good choices, they applauded her. The church became her family and remained family even after she'd moved into "The City" and backslid a bit.

That little girl grew to be one of my favorite people. Today she is Dr. Valerie Carter, alongside whom I served when she was Associate Pastor for Glocal (Global + Local) Ministries at our church. Now she is the Executive Director of Woman's Missionary Union of Virginia. Valerie has made a deep and eternal difference in the lives of countless people. She has helped people off the streets and off drugs and into the family of God. She constantly inspires people around her to get off their fannies and do something. Largely because her own life was transformed in a little church alongside the railroad tracks.

Dr. Carter's story is just one of countless stories about the power of the Church. You probably have your own story and know untold others. I tell that story up front because, frankly, some of us need to be reminded that, when we get it right, the Church is a beautiful thing. The Church, including that congregation you serve, is nothing less than "the church of God, which he bought with his own blood" (Acts 20:28).

Nevertheless, that church, including the one you serve, is a flawed institution in major transition. Its direction is unclear and its past has some skeletons. God's mission to the world is largely dependent upon a rather frail bunch of humans. The good news is, that's nothing new.

The Church in Transition

Part of our struggle is that the Western Church is in a major transition.

Alister Brown, President of Northern Seminary, once said, "Being in church is a bit like sitting in a sturdy boat in the river just upstream from Niagara Falls! The boat seems sound. And it is comfortable. All the while the water beneath the boat is rushing rapidly toward the precipice!"

Every five hundred years the Church undergoes a major shift—thus says Phyllis Tickle in her book *The Great Emergence*.

She quotes Mark Dyer, who says that every 500 years the Church has a giant rummage sale. I never had thought about it like that but it is absolutely right.

The Church was born in the first century A.D. Five hundred years later came Pope Gregory I and the emergence of the monastic movement. The monastic movement embodied the best of the Church and shaped it. This marked a big change in the Church.

Around the year 1000 (1054 to be exact) there was the Great Schism—the big division of the Church into East and West, with the Eastern Orthodox (now often called "Greek Orthodox") being centered in Constantinople (today's Istanbul) and the Western branch being based in Rome. The Church would forever be changed by that.

Then around the year 1500 there was the Protestant Reformation. There was a wind of revolution in the air already, with the new interest in intellectual pursuits known as the "Renaissance" sweeping Europe about that time. Yet the Reformation was one of the great watersheds of history. The result was the Protestant branch of Christianity and the genuine reformation of Roman Catholicism.

Today we are just beyond A.D. 2000, and our era's shift has been going on for several years. Science didn't solve all our problems, as so many thought it would. An emphasis on reason was replaced by a desire for experience. World War II ended with atomic bombs on Hiroshima and Nagasaki. The Sixties happened. Vietnam happened. The Berlin Wall fell. Along came the Internet. With all that, postmodernism was born.

The arrival of postmodernity has us all wondering what the future church is going to look like. It is a time of transition; we are between eras. As a church leader, I often felt like I was standing on a lake with one foot in one boat and the other foot in another boat. It's a bit wobbly. Unsteady. Uncertain. Even volatile. People are on edge. Strategies are imprecise—much like you would expect from people who have wandered into an area so unexplored even our GPS is of no help.

Discontinuity and Hope

Lyle Schaller wrote a book about the future of the Church titled *Discontinuity and Hope*. I think that title sums up the future of the Church in America.

The church of my grandchildren won't look like my church. I'm certain that the Church will experience more of a change over the next two decades than it has over the last century. If, twenty years from now, you see a church that looks like you remember church from the 1950s, look fast, for it will be shrinking by the day.

Yet I don't despair over the future of the Church. I have great hope. The power may shift (probably already has) to the Two-Thirds World. Worship styles, the size of worship centers, the delivery of theological education, the forms of congregational life, the role of denominations, all will change. Discontinuity indeed. Despite all the uncertainty, however, I see great hope for the future of Christ's Church.

Of Course, the Church Can Be Discouraging

While there is hope for the Church's future, it is still true that it can be a place of struggle, hurt, and discouragement. I love Phillip Gulley's novels about the little church in the little town of Harmony. One of my favorite tales of that congregation (whose members you would recognize from your own congregation if you were to read the stories) is of their goal-setting Sunday.

> The first Goal-Setting Sunday was held in 1970, the year Pastor Taylor came to Harmony fresh from seminary, chock-full of grand ideas... In 1970, their goals were, one, to spread the gospel to every tribe and person in the world, two, to end world hunger, and, three, to carpet the Sunday School rooms.
>
> They'd carpeted the Sunday school rooms first, donated a box of canned goods to the food pantry, and then lost their enthusiasm to do anything more.
>
> Goal-Setting Sunday had gone downhill from there, each year a stark testimony to the growing apathy of the church.[1]

Apathy has choked the life out of lots of really good church goals and strategic plans. And the church you serve might be more willing to carpet the Sunday school rooms than to take bold, world-changing, awe-inspiring steps. Serving and leading a passive passel of Christians can suck the life out of a pastor.

But often it's worse than mere apathy and pettiness. Often much worse.

The Church killed Christians in the Inquisition and Muslims in the Crusades, both in the name of Jesus, the Prince of Peace and Head of the Church. Church people have defended racism and ignored poverty. Since our beginnings we have been hypocritical and judgmental.

Churches claim to be family, but sometimes the only way we are like family is that we fight like brothers and sisters. We claim to be welcoming, but often prove to be welcoming only of those who look like we do. We claim to be a place where grace is the order of the day, then condemn people with a loathing that is embarrassing. I've lost count of the folks I've met who gave church a chance but were hurt by its people. And I think wounds inflicted by the church hurt worse and scar more deeply, for we expect more from Christians.

Still...

Even given the Church's flaws, I still contend that bashing, dismissing, or disowning the Church is not smart.

I've heard ministers declare the following about mean-spirited people in the congregation: "They can say what they want to about *me*, but when they start abusing *my spouse* they've crossed a line." Maybe you've said that. Maybe you've experienced more hurt over the pain your spouse has suffered than over the pain you have suffered personally.

I don't want to speak for God, but is it possible that He feels that way about His Church? Is it possible that God experiences a particularly profound pain when we bash, dismiss, or abandon His Church, His "bride"?

A friend of mine has experienced terrible treatment at the hand of his mother. Yet he respects her. He acknowledges her flaws without demonizing her. He refuses to disregard her although he now cuts short his visits when she is abusive. He chooses to love her when loving her is hard. Is there a lesson here too? I'd say so. Never dishonor your spiritual mother, the Church.

St. Augustine's profane words about the Church are quoted often: "The Church is a whore, but she's still my mother." I understand his sentiment, yet I flinch at his language about Christ's church, my "mother."

Nobody wins when we are naïve about a difficult congregation. Yet there does seem to be a line, the crossing of which puts us on thin ice. When skepticism becomes cynicism, when critical analysis becomes vilification, when discouragement becomes disparagement, that line has been crossed.

Some day it might be right—even the will of God—for you to move to a vocation other than that of being a minister in the Church. It's one thing to follow the prompting of God's Spirit to another role. It's quite another thing to walk out on the Church in either a temper tantrum or a pity party. It's a serious thing to attack, write off, or renounce the Church which God "bought with his own blood."

"...which he bought with his own blood"

For God, the Church was not an afterthought, a little extra He threw into the mix. It was not a superfluous little bonus. God paid for it with His own blood.

Serious students of the Greek New Testament disagree on the particularities of Paul's message here. Did Paul intend to say that God gave *His own* blood to acquire/establish the Church, or was it that God acquired/established the Church through *the blood of His own*, as in "His own Son"? It depends on how one translates *dia tou haimatos tou idiou*. Is it "which he bought with his own blood," as the NIV has it, or "that he obtained with the blood of his own Son," as the NRSV has it? It's a worthy question.

I've looked at the works of leading theologians and New Testament scholars and have had nothing short of a worship experience. To consider seriously the mystery of this phrase ("which he bought with his own blood") is to drill down into the fathomless sea of the Divine Unknown. To ponder such mystery is to worship the Almighty—He Who is beyond our boxes and imaginations. Charles Wesley said it beautifully: "Amazing love, how can it be? That Thou, my God, shouldst die for me?"

Either way—"bought with his own blood" or "with the blood of his own"—we are brought into the mystery of the Trinity. Either way—whether God bought the Church with His own blood, or God bought the Church with the blood of His own"—we are considering the Incarnation—God-in-the-flesh dwelling among us.

Acts 20:28 is one of those weighty and mystical references to Atonement—that multi-faceted, multi-effectual event which did more good for the world than we can fathom. Somehow, when Jesus bowed his head and declared, "It is finished," the future and mission of the Church had been secured. Perhaps G. Campbell Morgan said it best when he spoke of "the Church, redeemed by His blood, that is the blood of Christ, and in that sense, the very blood of God."[2]

God the Son, the Second Person of the Trinity, had died not only *on behalf of* the Church, but somehow to establish its purpose and very existence. This is no less than the theological underpinning of the Church we serve.

Wesley once more provides words that express my heart better than my own words can:

'Tis mystery all: th' Immortal dies!
Who can explore his strange design?
In vain the firstborn seraph tries
to sound the depths of love divine.
'Tis mercy all! Let earth adore;
let angel minds inquire no more.[3]

The Church and God's Redemption Plan

The Church is God's plan for redeeming the world. God's mission to the world always has included a people He would call His own. We rugged individualists in the United States have a harder time understanding that than most Christians around the globe do. But God always had a people in mind when He engaged His world. Originally it was the people of Israel. Certainly, He worked through individuals such as Abraham, Moses, and David. But the point always was the community, the family, the people movement. The same is true in and after the days of Jesus. Jesus founded the Church. His vision beyond his life on earth is of the Church. God is not surprised by the Church's flaws, yet the Church has always been at the heart of His plans.

Wherever the good news of Jesus spread in the New Testament, the result was a *congregation*, not lone rangers. Never did God envision isolated individuals trying to live out His purposes. He always had in mind a *people.*

You and I were born into a family when we were born anew. We were not intended to live in isolation. Jesus died not only to give individuals new lives but to create a new community where we will belong, find deep relationships, and use our passions and gifts for God's purposes.

Jesus didn't found a series of individual shrines; he founded the Church.

The Church, with all its scars and imperfections, still is the body of Christ and the institution that offers the most hope for the world. So I gladly and intentionally remain in this imperfect family, by my presence insuring that it will remain imperfect. I recommend, and believe in, the body of Christian believers.

And despite its flaws, the Church has been the most influential movement for good in history. We owe our Western educational system to the Church, who founded the early universities in Europe and the United States. We owe the freedom of Eastern Europe largely to the Church there. Oh, I know economic and political forces deserve a lot of the credit for that. But it was the candlelight vigils and imprisoned pastors in Romania and across Eastern Europe who changed the course of Communist Europe's history. We owe the abolition of slavery, the rise of orphanages, the eradication of the killing of twins in animistic cultures, and countless other societal advances to the Church. God has used the Church through the centuries, despite our scars and flaws, for immeasurable good.

Individuals can do wonderful things. But no one person can do what a church can do.

Nonprofit entities can do admirable things. But only the Church offers the grace and love and power of God to transform lives. Government programs can provide necessary assistance for people in need, because they have the power of the mayor, county officials, the governor, or the president behind them. Governmental agencies cannot rival the Church, however, for local congregations have the power of the Redeemer behind us.

The Church is imperfect. At our worst, we are a hypocritical, judgmental, out-of-touch, ingrown, country-clubish, bickering collection of folks who look little like Jesus. But at our best we reflect, if only in small ways, what the world would look like if God's will were done on earth as it is in Heaven.

Many people inside the Church show painfully little difference from people outside the Church. The overhead of many churches is appalling and hinders our mission, and sometimes people outside the church are nicer than people inside the church. But it still is the Church of God, and Jesus died for it. That includes even poor representatives of the Church like me. And there is the potential for genuine and holistic life-transformation in the Church that exists nowhere else.

When we get it right, in fact, the Church is a beautiful thing.

When we get it right, the Church is a place where people not only hear about God and sing about God but also *experience* God.

When we get it right the Church is a place where people who have been abused by their biological families find real family.

When we get it right, the Church is a place where people with hurts, habits, and hang-ups find both acceptance and answers.

When we get it right, the Church is a place where people looking for truth can come and ask questions without being ridiculed for asking, and they can actually find the truth they're seeking.

When we get it right, the Church is a place where people trying desperately to follow Jesus, and finding that an extremely lonely role, come and find community and know that they aren't alone.

When we get it right, Church is a place where people who are headed for a forever without God beyond this life find the incomparable assurance of a new eternal destiny—a place called "heaven"—by their faith in Jesus.

When we get it right, the Church is a beautiful thing.

We just don't always get it right.

After twenty years in pastoral ministry, Chip Bishop left the pastorate to become a financial advisor. I know Chip, and I know his character and reasoning to be admirable. In an interview about his transition to the financial world, Chip made an insightful statement: "Two quotes seem to capture the poles on either side of the tight wire we balance upon in church ministry and in my own walk with Jesus: 'I would accept Christ if he did not insist on dragging along that leprous bride,' by William Southey and, conversely, 'There is so much that the church does right that is not done by anybody else,' by William Willimon."[4]

Let's Love the Church

We can't get away from the truth that sometimes it's hard to love the Church. Living in community is hard, and a faith community is no exception. Churches of all stripes have issues. While the Lord of the Church is perfect, the people of the Church are not.

I would not have written this book if I were unaware of the Church's serious blemishes and if I didn't know unbelievably unchristian stories of clergy maltreatment. However, deep in my heart, I love and believe in the Church.

The Church is still the body of Christ, bought by the blood of God-in-the-flesh. Immanuel died not only to redeem you, but also to redeem your congregation. The Church is not synonymous with the Kingdom of God, but the Church—including that congregation you serve—is God's primary vehicle for the expansion of that Kingdom.

In 2004 our Roman Catholic friends were reeling from the child abuse scandals triggered by the institutional cover-up of the actions of a few priests who violated children, defied their vows, and soiled the Church's name. In the January 5, 2004 issue of *Newsweek,* there appeared an article about Rev. Wilton Gregory, president of the U.S. Conference of Catholic Bishops and a leading spokesperson for the Catholic Church in America. Bishop Gregory had been forced to defend the church in legal documents, courtrooms, and the court of public opinion. I'm certain he bore a heavy weight in his heart. Yet he said he never "ceased to believe this is Christ's church." He continued: "It's wounded. It's sinful. It's humiliated. But it's Christ's church, and I'm glad to be a bishop in this church." Bishop Gregory and I would have our differences. But on this matter I agree with him: *This is Christ's church. It's wounded. It's sinful. It's humiliated. But it's Christ's church. And I'm glad to be counted among the pastors in this church.*

A repentant spirit would be appropriate for people of *all* churches. The Church is tarnished and deserves to be held accountable for our sins—both by fellow humans and by God. Nevertheless, the Church is the hands and feet of Jesus. God has used the Church through the centuries, despite our scars and flaws, for immeasurable good. You and I have been on the receiving end of some really wonderful ministry from the Church.

From the last church I served as pastor, all the way back to the church into which I was born, I have been blessed by the people of the Church.

My first heroes, outside of my father, were at church.

My parents taught me a love for the Bible, but I learned its stories at church.

Young adults in the church I grew up in invested in me and mentored me.

Even my first kiss was in the fellowship hall after a Sunday evening service at church.

In 1976, when I was a senior in high school, I took my first paid church position as an Assistant Youth Director. I was called to that position because of my unquestionable skills—oh, and maybe because my uncle was the pastor. Every day since then, with the exception of a stretch of a few months when I was in college, I have been in the employ of the most important organization on earth—the Church.

I've led church youth groups and directed church music. I've served alongside career missionaries and Venezuelan leaders in Venezuelan churches. Then, as a career missionary myself in Nigeria, I taught in a seminary and preached in all kinds of churches. During our last year in Nigeria, I was the interim pastor of a church of lepers.

I've had the sacred honor of having the people of four great churches in Kentucky and Virginia call me "Pastor." And when I say "great churches," I'm not just fawning. I have been exceptionally blessed by the privilege to be among genuinely Christian people who meant more to me than I ever could to them.

I love the Church. Yes, that love is more than an emotion; it is a choice. Yet I love the Church, and I hope you will love Her, too.

…And Learn to Minister Differently

Someone compared the Church to Noah's ark. If it weren't for the conditions outside, it was said, the situation inside would be unbearable.

Even if you aren't ready to compare your congregation to the ark, my serious hunch is that many of you reading this are struggling somewhat to love the church. I understand that. One of the most important things I read during my dark days of near flameout was *pastorpain* by Steve Bagi. In this excerpt you can see the frustration some of you are feeling, or one day may feel:

"If we flick through the pages of the Bible we will soon see that it has never been an easy thing to be a leader in God's family. No significant leader mentioned in the Bible ever had a smooth run. Sometimes they stuffed it up themselves, but for the most part throughout history, God's leaders have struggled with the apathy, disobedience, sin, resistance to change and the lack of openness to His Spirit from His beloved little children… As I finished up in my pastoral role I couldn't help wondering if all the time and energy that I had poured into it was really worthwhile. Of course, so many great things have happened, but at the end of the day I still felt that I and my corner of churchworld had not made the impact that I would have hoped for… Now looking at the whole church scene from the outside, I cannot help noticing the disparity between input from in terms of man hours and money, compared to the output…which, in many places, is very few people becoming Christians.[5]

Later on in the same book, Bagi wrote about his decision to leave vocational ministry:

I couldn't lead anymore. It's not just because I was burned out, it was that I no longer believed in the show. My faith and love for Jesus is stronger than ever but somehow I fear that we have veered off the path. In my ministry, I have tried to help the church to grow and improve… I maintained and developed the system but the system has to change… I feel old inside and have fed the machine for too long to see the path clearly.[6]

It's easy for a pastor to feel like you're maintaining an institution instead of fueling a mission. Yet in my own life, and in the lives of others, I've noted how pastors can avoid that machine-feeding feeling.

Do what you're best at, and what only you can do. You might have to revise the organizational chart at your place, and you certainly will need buy-in from congregational leaders, but everyone will benefit if your ministry fits your gifts and passions.

Get outside the walls. Do your study at a local coffee shop, for example. Have intentional spiritual conversations with people who are far from God and almost certainly are not going to walk through the doors of your church building.

If you're going to begin a new church program, make it a program focused on people who aren't yet in your church. Ingrown churches, like toenails, are painful to live with.

Lead your church to launch a fresh expression[7] of church—a form of church that has all the elements of a church but looks nothing like your present congregation and measures success in ways other than nickels and noses.

Maybe most importantly (at least it was the most important thing for me), open your eyes to what God is doing through His Church. Listen to the stories; don't pass them off. Hear what people are saying about the transformation they are experiencing. Don't underestimate the life-transforming power of your ministry.

In my more cynical moments, I was certain my ministry was fruitless, and the church was nothing more than a nice club. In my more objective moments, however, I really did see the difference—often the eternal difference—that God was making in people's lives through the church I served as pastor. It was seeing that difference that helped strengthen my spirit and return me to a healthy place. Blind to the impact of my ministry, the challenges of ministry seemed overwhelming. So open your eyes and see what God is doing.

*****

A Closing Note to New Ministers

Our oldest son, Landon, was beginning to feel a calling to serve in a church as a youth pastor. While part of me was proud and even thrilled, another part of me was a bit nervous. So, during his Christmas break from college, I asked him to take an hour-and-a-half ride with me to Charlottesville, Virginia, where I was going to officiate at the graveside service of a deceased member.

We were barely out of Richmond when I began my spiel. "Landon," I said, "I want to make sure you know what you are getting into. This church thing is hard. Maybe you haven't witnessed that. First of all, your mom and I have been blessed to be in really healthy, wonderful churches. And when we were in Nigeria, we had a great situation and a great community of fellow missionaries and Nigerian Christian friends and co-workers. Second, when we have had problems, we haven't discussed them in front of you and your brother and sister. So, I'm afraid you are viewing church service through rose-colored glasses."

I went on to tell him that church people are people and sometimes they can be downright mean. I told him a couple of horror stories about ministers I've known. I told him how rewarding ministry can be, and how he can play a deeply satisfying role in genuine life transformation. When things get tough, however—and they will—I at least wanted him to be able to remember I had warned him.

So to those of you who are new to vocational church ministry, consider yourself warned, but hopefully not dissuaded. I would not point anyone away from vocational ministry. I simply believe you will serve more joyfully if you know what could be coming.

A Closing Note to Veterans of Vocational Ministry

For a couple of years before the publication of this book, a handful of us have been leading a workshop for pastors nearing burnout. We've called it "Staying in the Game." That is what I would want for you—that you stay in the game—that you remain true to the local church and to a biblical model of ministry and that you enjoy it.

Now, after resigning my position as pastor and assuming the role of consultant, I feel a little awkward asking you to remain in the local church. But I really want you to know this about me: I stayed in the game through the tough stretch. While I was a pastor I didn't receive any more inquiries from search committees than other pastors do, I'm sure. Yet, it always seemed that call from a search committee would come during a particularly difficult week. In fact, during the toughest week of my vocational ministry, a church called. I was so tempted to go. I went to their website and fantasized about what I was certain would be a serene congregation of people who were passionate to reach outsiders and ready to follow me wherever I'd lead them. Of course that was a fantasy, and to have gone to that church would have been unfair to everyone. And to have left at any time during the dark stretches would have been disobedient to God.

When I did finally leave, I left on a real upbeat. Ironically, the last year of my tenure was one of the best of the dozen years I was there. Though I sometimes questioned how a sane person could walk away at such a positive time, it felt good to leave at a healthy stage for myself and to leave the church in a good position.

Hear me: I know sometimes a minister has to leave during the bad times. In some cases it simply would be disastrous for everyone for a minister to stubbornly stick it out. In such cases, don't stay too long.

But don't leave too early, either.

Go back and review the material in chapter 5 and remember: Don't let go of the ski rope so quickly you don't give yourself time to "come up." But, on the other hand, don't hang on so long that the rope gets ripped from your white-knuckled hand or you drown.

Last Words

I grew up, as some of you did, watching westerns on TV. I have great memories of sitting with my dad in his easy chair watching *Gunsmoke* on Saturday nights. Usually on *Gunsmoke* and other westerns somebody got shot, bled ketchup, and died. Often the one shot would hang on just long enough to share something important with their last breaths. The outlaw would get shot and live just long enough for the marshal to get there so he could confess and tell where the money was hidden. The young wife, shot by a stray bullet, would live long enough for her husband to cradle her in his arms. "Make 'em pay, Johnny," she'd say. Then her head would fall limp on his chest.

And that doesn't happen only in TV westerns. In a couple's last moments together before a soldier ships out for the Middle East, when one's eighteen-year-old son or daughter gets in the car to drive five states away to attend college, or during one's final moments on earth, the last words are most likely going to be tender and significant.

When I was a little boy, Uncle Barto was my idol. All our major holidays were spent with him and his family. His two daughters were the only cousins I knew well, and our families were very close. Uncle Barto, a pastor, was about 6'3" with broad shoulders and a hearty laugh. He also had a bad heart. I remember well an occasion when his heart was so weak his very life was in danger. His heart had been weakened by the stress of church conflict. In fact, everybody thought the strain of that conflict was going to kill him. I did. He did, too. He *didn't* die; it was years later that his heart wore out. However, at the time, we thought he would soon depart this world.

During that illness, my Mom and I were visiting him when he asked to speak to me alone. I remember standing by his bedside. Frankly, I cannot remember exactly what he said, for I was a little fellow and probably scared to death. But I do remember the look in his eyes and the feel of that conversation. The mood was somber. The message was significant. I can still sense the gravity of his words even if I don't remember them. I remember knowing one thing—Uncle Barto was using what he thought might be our last conversation to say something to me of grave importance.

The apostle Paul was headed to Jerusalem where an almost certain arrest awaited. He declared, "Compelled by the Spirit, I am going to Jerusalem, not knowing what will happen to me there" (Acts 20:22). Soon he added, "I consider my life worth nothing to me; my only aim is to finish the race and complete the task the Lord Jesus has given me" (v. 24). Feel the emotion in these words: "When Paul had finished speaking, he knelt down with all of them and prayed. They all wept as they embraced him and kissed him. What grieved them most was his statement that they would never see his face again. Then they accompanied him to the ship" (vv. 36–38).

We know from Acts 21 that Paul was indeed arrested in Jerusalem. From there he was taken to Caesarea where he appeared before Felix, then Festus. Paul invoked his rights as a Roman citizen and appealed to Caesar. After an appearance before Agrippa, soon Paul was on a ship to Rome—not as a passenger but as a prisoner. The last we heard from Paul, he was under house arrest at the heart of the Roman Empire preaching to all who would hear.

My point is this: When one is nearing the end of one's life, or at least thinks one is, he or she doesn't waste breath and time on trivial matters. In his last conversation with people to whom Paul obviously felt very close, the apostle spoke of the Church. Paul, the erudite theologian and international missionary, spoke of life where-the-rubber-meets-the-road on the front lines of Kingdom advance—the Church. He didn't mince words. He didn't ignore hard realities. Yet he spoke with passion about the Church—its dangers, its mission, and its vocational ministry. There was nothing more important to Paul than local congregations and the universal Church. There was nothing more important to him than what you do and how you do it.

So be grateful for, and appropriately proud of, your calling. I understand the priesthood of all believers, but in our effort to declare that all Christians are ministers, we might have unintentionally devalued the responsibility and honor of the call to spend our lives and make our livings serving and leading the Church. Your calling is a special calling. What you do is of eternal significance.

Remember: You serve and lead the Church of God, which He bought with His blood.

Notes

CHAPTER 1: What You Do Is Hard

[1]Quoted in Anne Jackson, *Mad Church Disease* (Grand Rapids, Mich.: Zondervan, 2009), 85.

[2]From http://www.forbes.com/sites/robasghar/2014/02/25/ranking-the-9-toughest-leadership-roles.

[3]Quoted by William Willimon in *Changing Lives Through Preaching and Worship* (Grand Rapids, Mich.: Zondervan, 1995), 83.

[4]J. R. Woodward, *Creating a Missional Culture* (Downers Grove, Ill.: InterVarsity Press, 2012), 98.

[5]Gary L. Pinion, *Crushed: The Perilous Side of Ministry* (Springfield, Mo.: 21st Century Press, 2008), 10, 39, 57.

[6]Here are some more statistics:
* 80 percent of pastors feel discouraged.
* 45 percent say that they've experienced depression or burnout to the extent that they need to take a leave of absence from ministry.

For stats see Marcus N. Tanner and Anisa M. Zvonkovic, "Forced Termination of American Clergy: Its Effects and Connection to Negative Well-Being," *Review of Religious Research* (December, 2011); www.pastorburnout.com; Lance Witt, *Replenish* (Grand Rapids, Mich.: Baker Books, 2011), 18–19; Michael Todd Wilson and Brad Hoffman, *Preventing Ministry Failure* (Downers Grove, Ill.: InterVarsity Press, 2007), 31. See also Calvin Miller, *Letters to a Young Pastor* (Colorado Springs: David C. Cook, 2011), 50-52, and *Fail: Finding Hope and Grace in the Midst of Ministry Failure* (Downers Grove, Ill.: InterVarsityPress, 2014).

[7]Here's what Paul Vitello said in *The New York Times*: "The findings have surfaced with ominous regularity over the last few years, and with little notice: Members of the clergy now suffer from obesity, hypertension and depression at rates higher than most Americans. In the last decade, their use of antidepressants has risen, while their life expectancy has fallen. Many would change jobs if they could." ("Taking a Break from the Lord's Work," *The New York Times*, August 1, 2010). See also Miller, *Letters to a Young Pastor*, 50–52.

[8]Sheri S. Ferguson, "Clergy Compassion Fatigue," *Family Therapy Magazine* (March/April 2007): 16.

[9]The precipitous decline in trust for leaders and institutions has been documented in lots of studies. One of the most sobering is the 2013 Edelman Trust Barometer, which notes how little people trust leaders of all kinds. (See www.scribd.com/doc/121501475/Executive-Summary-2013-Edelman-Trust-Barometer). Also, a December 2013 Gallup Poll noted specifically the decline of trust in religious leaders. Their article/report was titled "Honesty and Ethics Rating of Clergy Slides to New Low."

[10]Peter Steinke, *Congregational Leadership in Anxious Times* (Herndon, Va.: Alban, 2006), 101.

[11]Ruth Gledhill wrote: "A bishop is among the 150 clergy and ministers who have sought protection with the trade union Unite from what it describes as a culture of bullying in the established Church... The union, which has set up a special helpline for priests intimidated by their bishops or congregations, is reviewing its clergy caseload as part of its campaign for full employment rights for clergy." Ruth Gledhill, "Clergy and Ministers Need Protection from Church Bullying, Unite Union Says," copyright BishopAccountability.org, 2004, http://www.bishop-accountability.org/news2010/01_02/2010_01_04_Gledhill_ClergyAnd.htm.

Pastor bullying—along with other sorts of bullying—is a phenomenon undergoing a resurgence. "It has resurfaced, perhaps, because of the political climate. We're more polarized than ever," [Susan] Nienaber [of the Alban Institute] said. "But in the more than 20 years I've been a consultant, I've seen an increase in incivility over the years—although congregations are notorious for what they're willing to tolerate in the name of being a Christian community. The healthiest congregations have the lowest tolerance for inappropriate behavior. Unhealthy congregations tolerate the most outrageous behavior." Julie B. Sevig, "Bullying the Pastor," *The Lutheran* (February 2011) (see thelutheran.org.).

I ran across two other articles on pastors being bullied. The first is by Martin Shankleman, "Clergy Bullying Rife," John Mark Ministries, 2010 (http://jmm.aaa. net.au/articles/23204.htm). See also Kristina Drumheller, "The Bullied Pulpit: The Church as a Site for Workplace Bullying," 2009 (http://connection.ebscohost.com/c/articles/54435208/bullied-pulpit-church-as-site-workplace-bullying).

[12]See, for example, *The American Church Research Project, 2010* (www. TheAmericanChurch.org). See also *The Great Decline: 60 years of religion in one graph* (at religionnews.com).

[13]See "The End of Christian America," *Newsweek* (April 8, 2009).

[14]I gained this insight from John and Sylvia Ronsvalle's book, *Behind the Stained Glass Windows* (Grand Rapids, Mich.: Baker Books, 1996), 57–63.

[15]Kathleen Smith, *Stilling the Storm: Worship and Congregational Leadership in Difficult Times* (Herndon, Va.: The Alban Institute, 2006), 146–47.

[16]"National Congregational Study," *Review of Religious Research*. In *Christianity Today*, vol. 56, no. 5 (May 2012): 9.

[17]Jay Gilbert, "The Millennials: A new generation of employees, a new set of engagement policies," *The Workplace* (September / October 2011).

[18]Speed Leas, *Leading Your Church Through Conflict and Reconciliation* (Minneapolis: Bethany House, 1997), 53.

[19]Ministers aren't the only ones who get hurt by the church, by the way. David Bosch wrote, "Every church member who loves the church will also be deeply pained by it." In *Transforming Mission* (Maryknoll, N.Y.: Orbis Books, 396).

[20]From http://www.csmonitor.com/Photo-Galleries/In-Pictures/The-10-happiest-jobs (2011)

CHAPTER 2: There and Back

[1]Gordon MacDonald, *Who Stole My Church?* (Nashville: Thomas Nelson, 2007), 224.

[2]See 2 Corinthians 12:7–10.

[3]"The word 'elder' is *presbutos* in the Greek ('presbyter') and refers to a mature person who has been selected to serve in office (Acts 14:23). These same people are called 'overseers' in Acts 20:28, which is *episkopos* or 'bishop.' They were chosen to 'feed the church' (Acts 20:28), which means 'to shepherd.' Paul called the local church 'a flock' (Acts 20:28–29), so these men were also pastors. (The word *pastor* means 'shepherd.') Thus in the New Testament churches, the three titles, *elder, bishop* and *pastor,* were synonymous." (Warren Wiersbe, *The Bible Exposition Commentary* [Wheaton, Ill.: Victor Books, 1989], 486). In his commentary on this Acts 20:28 text, C. H. C. Macgregor noted in *The Interpreter's Bible* (Nashville: Abingdon Press, 1954), 273, that "'overseers' here is synonymous with 'shepherd.'" Furthermore, it says in Acts 20:18 that Paul called the *elders* together. So in Acts 20:18 and 28 the same people are referred to as elders, overseers, and pastors/shepherds. T. C. Smith states it like this: "Luke does not make a distinction between elders and bishops as the Christians of the second century A. D. did. The *presbueroi* (elders) are the same as *episkopoi* (guardians, bishops, or overseers)…" ("Acts," *The Broadman Bible Commentary* [Nashville: Broadman Press, 1970], 119). See also George Eldon Ladd, *A Theology of the New Testament* (Grand Rapids, Mich.: William B. Eerdmans, 1974), 352, 532.

[4]"Paul's speech to the Ephesian elders would be a fine text for an ordination sermon or for a reconstruction of our theology of ordination. In its interplay between the *action* and the *being* of church leaders, its focus is upon the *duties* of the elders for the support, care, and protection of the flock, in its frank admission for the *possibilities for pain* within the

Christian ministry it provides us with a model (as Paul himself was a model) for thinking about Christian ministry." (William Willimon, "Acts," in *Interpretation Commentary* [Atlanta: John Knox Press, 1988], 158).

CHAPTER 3: Keep Watch

[1]Bill Self, *Defining Moments* (Lima, Ohio: CSS Publishing, 1999), 37.

[2]William Barclay, *The Acts of the Apostles* (Philadelphia: Westminster Press, 1976), 151.

[3]Walter Bauer, *A Greek-English Lexicon of the New Testament* (Chicago: The University of Chicago Press, 1957), 714.

[4]W. O. Carver, *Acts of the Apostles* (Nashville: Broadman Press, 1916), 205.

[5]Greg Warner, "When pastors' silent suffering turns tragic," *USA Today*, October 28, 2009. Also from that article: "Being a pastor—a high-profile, high-stress job with nearly impossible expectations for success—can send one down the road to depression, according to pastoral counselors... 'The likelihood is that one out of every four pastors is depressed,' said Matthew Stanford, a professor of psychology and neuroscience at Baylor University in Waco, Texas... 'But anxiety and depression in the pulpit are "markedly higher" in the last five years,' said [Fred] Smoot (Director of Emory Clergy Care in Duluth, Ga.). 'The current economic crisis has caused many of our pastors to go into depression. Besides the recession's strain on church budgets, depressed pastors increasingly report frustration over their congregations' resistance to cultural change.'"

[6]Daniel Sherman, *Pastor Burnout Workbook* (e-book, PastorBurnout.com, 2011), 8, 16.

[7]Richard Kriegbaum, *Leadership Prayers* (Carol Stream, Ill.: Tyndale House, 1998), 56.

[8]Steve Bagi, *pastorpain: my journey in burnout* (e-book, Palm Beach, Queensland, Australia: Actuate Consulting, 2008), 24; Also consider: "Virtually nobody knows what we do—not our congregations, not the community, very often not the professors who taught us, not even (and this is the most unsettling) the bishops and executives and superintendents who provide overall direction and counsel to our work... In society, nonrecognition is comparable. Our vocation made us invisible. A pastor in America is the invisible man, the invisible woman." (Eugene Peterson, *The Pastor* [New York: Harper One, 2011], 146, 147).

[9]National Congregation Study, 2006–2007, cited in "Killing the Clergy Softly: Congregational Conflict, Job Loss and Depression" (The Association of Religious Data Archives). See http://blogs.thearda.com/trend/religion/killing-the-clergy-softly-congregational-conflict-job-loss-and-depression.

[10]Guy Greenfield, *The Wounded Minister* (Grand Rapids, Mich.: Baker Books, 2001), 13, 14.

[11]Gary L. McIntosh and Samuel D. Rima, *Overcoming the Dark Side of Leadership: How to Become an Effective Leader by Confronting Potential Failures* (Grand Rapids, Mich.: Baker Books, 2007).

[12]The term *self-differentiation* originated in the field of biology. A self-differentiated cell cooperates with other cells, yet is self-sufficient. The basic concept of self-differentiation has since been developed and applied to human leadership studies.

[13]I especially recommend the following works by Edwin H. Friedman: *A Failure of Nerve* (New York: Seabury Books, 2007); *Generation to Generation* (New York: The Guilford Press, 1985); and *Congregational Leadership in Anxious Times* (Lanham, Md.: Rowman & Littlefield, 2006).

[14]Wayne Cordeiro, *Leading on Empty* (Minneapolis: Bethany House, 2009), 11.

[15]Richard Foster, *Celebration of Discipline* (New York: Harper Collins, 1978), 1.

[16]Gordon MacDonald, *The Life God Blesses* (Nashville: Thomas Nelson, 1994), 70.

[17]Barbara Brown Taylor, *Leaving Church* (San Francisco: Harper San Francisco, 2006), 111.

[18]Lillian Daniel and Martin B. Copenhavor, *This Odd & Wondrous Calling* (Grand Rapids, Mich.: William B. Eerdmans, 2009), 58.

[19]Henri J. Nouwen, *In the Name of Jesus: Reflections on Christian Leadership* (New York: Crossroad, 1989).

[20]J. Oswald Sanders, *Spiritual Leadership* (Chicago: Moody Press, 1967), 102.

[21]Marshall Shelley, in *Leading Your Church Through Conflict and Reconciliation,* Marshall Shelley, general editor (Minneapolis: Bethany House, 1997), 67.

[22]Bill Hybels, *Honest to God* (Grand Rapids, Mich.: Zondervan, 1990), 170.

[23]Charles Chandler, "Forced Termination Leaves Deep Scars on Ministers' Spouses," (unpublished paper).

[24]Quoted in John Maxwell, *Developing the Leader Within You* (Nashville: Thomas Nelson Publishers, 1993), 161.

[25]Stephen Covey, *First Things First* (New York: Simon & Schuster, 1994), 105, 112.

[26]Calvin Miller, *Letters to a Young Pastor* (Colorado Springs: David C. Cook, 2011), 125.

[27]Bill Self, *Surviving the Stained Glass Jungle* (Macon, Ga.: Mercer University Press, 2011), 40.

CHAPTER 4: All the Flock

[1]Lillian Daniel and Martin B. Copenhaver, *This Odd and Wondrous Calling* (Grand Rapids, Mich.: William B. Eerdmans, 2009) , 63.

[2]Robert E. Webber, *Younger Evangelicals* (Grand Rapids, Mich.: Baker Books, 2002), 52.

[3]Peter Scazzero, *The Emotionally Healthy Church* (Grand Rapids, Mich.: Zondervan, 2010), 134.

[4]"Most ministers I know would testify that fewer than 10 percent of their members ever say cutting things or behave unkindly toward them in any way. Many congregants are generous, loving people and want to make their pastors and their families as happy and comfortable as possible... But sometimes a minister under fire can feel as if the numbers are reversed, and it is 90 percent of the people who are after his or her hide, while only 10 percent behave with decency and civility." (John Killinger, *Seven Things They Don't Tell You in Seminary* [New York: Crossroad, 2006], 130).

[5]Maurice Graham, e-mail dated February 28, 2014.

[6]In Arthur Paul Boers, *Never Call Them Jerks* (Washington, D.C.: Alban Institute, 1999), 119.

[7]William Willimon, *The Collected Sermons of William H. Willimon* (Louisville: Westminster John Knox Press, 2010), 183.

[8]Steve Bagi, *pastorpain: my journey in burnout* (e-book, Palm Beach, Queensland, Australia: Actuate Consulting, 2008), 37–39.

[9]Eugene Peterson, *Under the Unpredictable Plant* (Grand Rapids, Mich.: William B. Eerdmans, 1992), 17.

[10]Anne Jackson, *Mad Church Disease* (Grand Rapids: Zondervan, 2009), 168.

[11]Donald T. Phillips, *Lincoln on Leadership* (New York: Warner Books, 1992), 27–33.

[12]Richard Kriegbaum, *Leadership Prayers* (Carol Steam, Ill.: Tyndale House, 1998), 64.

[13]Scott Peck, *People of the Lie* (New York: Simon & Schuster, 1983), 68.

CHAPTER 5: The Call

[1]Ben Patterson, *Leading Your Church Through Conflict and Reconciliation,* Marshall Shelley, general editor (Minneapolis: Bethany House, 1997), 21.

[2]Dietrich Bonhoeffer, *Cost of Discipleship* (New York: Touchstone, 1995), 206.

[3]Jake Colson, *So You Don't Want To Go To Church Anymore* (Los Angeles: Windblown Media, 2006), 161–65.

[4]The *COMPASS* originally appeared in my book *Directionally Challenged* (Birmingham: New Hope, 2006).

[5]Richard Foster, *Celebration of Discipline: The Path to Spiritual Growth* (San Francisco: Harper & Row, 1978).

[6]John Killinger, *Seven Things They Don't Teach You in Seminary* (New York: Crossroad, 2006), 147–57.

[7]Ibid, 159–60.

[8]Eugene Peterson, *Under the Unpredictable Plant* (Grand Rapids. Mich.: William B. Eerdmans, 1992), 18–19.

[9]Ibid., 28–29.

[10]Quoted in John Ortberg, *If You Want to Walk on Water, You've Got to Get Out of the Boat* (Grand Rapids, Mich.: Zondervan, 2001), 103.

[11]Martin Luther King, Jr., *The Papers of Martin Luther King, Jr. Volume VI*, Clayborne Carson, Senior Editor (Berkley: University of California Press, 2007), 280.

[12]Ruth Haley Barton, *Pursuing God's Will Together* (Downers Grove, Ill.: InterVarsity Press, 2012), 63.

[13]Warren Wiersbe, *Be Obedient* (Wheaton, Ill.: Victor Books, 1991), 55.

[14]Robert Schuller, *Tough Times Never Last, But Tough People Do* (Nashville: Thomas Nelson, 1983), 179–80.

[15]Ted Traylor, "Water from Home," *Leadership Journal* (Fall, 2004). http://www.christianitytoday.com/le/2004/fall/19.43.html.

[16]Gordon MacDonald, *Who Stole My Church?* (Nashville: Thomas Nelson, 2007), 224.

CHAPTER 6: Overseers with Authority

[1]Steve Bagi, *pastorpain: my journey in burnout* (e-book, Palm Beach, Queensland, Australia: Actuate Consulting, 2008), 37–39.

[2]Bill Self, *Surviving the Stained Glass Jungle* (Macon, Ga.: Mercer University Press, 2011), 85–86, 88.

[3]J. Oswald Sanders, *Spiritual Leadership* (Chicago: Moody Press, 1994), 113.

[4]Joseph Girzone, *Joshua* (New York: Macmillan, 1987), 89. In David Bosch's magnum opus, *Transforming Mission*, he stated the following: "[M]any evangelical denominations which tend to follow a congregational polity, are struggling to avoid one of two pitfalls; either the minister becomes a little pope whose word is law or the congregation regards him as their employee who has to dance to their tune." (Maryknoll, N.Y.: Orbis Books, 2012), 481.

[5]Peter L. Steinke, *Congregational Leadership in Anxious Times* (Herndon, VA.: Alban, 2006), 139.

[6]See, for example, Robert Webber, *The Younger Evangelicals* (Grand Rapids, Mich.: Baker Books, 2002), 149, 153.

[7]J. R. Woodward, *Creating a Missional Culture* (Downers Grove, Ill.: InterVarsity Press, 2012), 65, 105. See also p. 221.

[8]Bill Easum, in *The Church of the Perfect Storm*, Leonard Sweet, ed. (Nashville: Abingdon Press, 2008), 94.

[9]Ibid.

[10]"Because a minister is an authority figure, he may become autocratic in his relationships. He may fall into the trap of assuming that his every whim should be viewed as a pronouncement from Mt. Sinai. Moreover, the minister is often encouraged to be autocratic. Some members feel more comfortable with a father figure who will tell them what they should do and/or believe. They look forward to receiving a verbal 'spanking' every week. If they can come to church and have the pastor fuss at them and spank them for their shortcomings, they can leave the worship service without the painful process of confession and acceptance of forgiveness. They accept verbal spanking as atonement for the sins which they have committed.

"While being autocratic may have some benefits for preaching, it plays havoc with the process of being 'fellow workers' of Christ. An autocratic minister does not easily accept criticism and suggestions from the members of the congregation. He is frequently defensive, and when confronted with significant opposition, he often lashes out at those who dare to question his judgment. Such behavior hinders members from offering their suggestions and recommendations to the pastor. Consequently, the ministry of the church is diminished because it becomes a 'one-man-show.' In turn, the spirit of the congregation suffers because there is no opportunity to negotiate differences. An autocratic minister also has difficulty working with staff members." (Edward Bratcher, *The Walk on Water Syndrome* [Waco: Word, 1984], 33–34).

[11]Reggie McNeal, *A Work of Heart* (San Francisco: Jossey-Bass, 2000), 158.

[12]Gottfried Osei-Mensah, *Wanted: Servant Leaders* (Achimota, Ghana: African Christian Press, 1996), 20.

[13]Lillian Daniel and Martin B. Copenhaver, *This Odd and Wondrous Calling* (Grand Rapids, Mich.: William B. Eerdmans, 2009), 5.

[14]Joe McKeever, "This Pastor Gives 100 Tips for Leaders That Everyone in Ministry Should Know," http://www.churchleaders.com/pastors/pastor-articles/170770-joe-mckeever-pastor-gives-100-tips-for-leaders-that-everyone-in-ministry-should-know.html.

[15]Sanders, *Spiritual Leadership*, 153.

[16]George Bullard, "What If It Really Is the Pastor's Fault?" A Travel Free Learning Article; The Columbia Partnership, May 22, 2012.

[17]McKeever, "100 Tips."

[18]Daniel Sherman, *Pastor Burnout Workbook* (e-book, 2011), 34–35.

CHAPTER 7: Shepherds vs. Hired Hands

[1]Jon McIntosh, ChurchLeaders.com, "6 Reasons Why Pastors Want to Quit on Mondays"; http://www.churchleaders.com/pastors/pastor-articles/150317-jon-mcintosh-six-reasons-why-pastors-want-to-quit-on-mondays.html

[2]Marilynne Robinson, *Gilead* (New York: Picador, 2004), 70.

[3]Lynn Anderson, *They Smell Like Sheep* (West Monroe, La.: Howard Publishing, 1997), 34.

[4]Bill Hull, *The Disciple-Making Pastor* (Grand Rapids, Mich.: Fleming H. Revell, 1988), 75–76.

[5]Alan C. Klaas, Cheryl D. Klaas, *Quiet Conversations* (Kansas City: Mission Growth Publishing, 2000), 24–25, 69.

[6]Tim Clark, correspondence.

[7]Calvin Miller, *Letters to a Young Pastor* (Colorado Springs: David C. Cook, 2011), 84.

[8]Richard Baxter, quoted in ibid., 84–85. I'm confused by Miller's advice, by the way, since he served for many years as pastor of a church with well over 2,000 members.

[9]Eugene H. Peterson, *Under the Unpredictable Plant: An Exploration of Vocational Holiness* (Grand Rapids, Mich.: William B. Eerdmans, 1992), 135.

[10]William Webb, *Slaves, Women and Homosexuals: Exploring the Hermeneutics of Cultural Analysis* (Downers Grove, Ill., InterVarsity Press, 2001), 60.

[11]Laurie Beth Jones, *Jesus CEO* (New York: Hyperion, 1994), 180.

[12]Quoted in Arthur Paul Boers, *Never Call Them Jerks* (Washington, D.C.: Alban Institute, 1999), 118.

[13]Dietrich Bonhoeffer, *Life Together* (New York: Harper & Row, 1954), 29–30.

[14]Quoted in William H. Willimon, *Collected Sermons of William H. Willimon* (Louisville: Westminster John Knox Press, 2011), 100.

[15]I recommend the following books in preparation for these talks: Kerry Patterson, Joseph Grenny, Ron McMillan, and Al Switzler, *Crucial Conversations: Tools for Talking When the Stakes Are High* (New York: McGraw-Hill, 2002); Kerry Patterson, Joseph Grenny, Ron McMillan and Al Switzler, *Crucial Confrontation: Tools for Resolving Broken Promises, Violated Expectations, and Bad Behavior* (New York: McGraw-Hill, 2005); and Henry Cloud and John Townsend, *How To Have That Difficult Conversation You've Been Avoiding* (Grand Rapids, Mich.: Zondervan, 2003).

[16]Tom Blackaby, *Experiencing God's Love* (Birmingham: New Hope Publishers, 2011), 14.

[17]Kathleen S. Smith, *Stilling the Storm: Worship and Congregational Leadership in Difficult Times* (Herndon, Va.: Alban, 2006), 192.

CHAPTER 8: The Church of God

[1]Philip Gulley, *Just Shy of Harmony* (New York: HarperCollins, 2002), 3.

[2]G. Campbell Morgan, *The Acts of the Apostles* (Old Tappan, N.J.: Fleming H. Revell, 1924), 472.

[3]Charles Wesley, *And Can It Be That I Should Gain?*, 1738.

[4]Chip Bishop, *Interview with Chip Bishop, On Changing from Senior Pastor to Financial Advisor: A Conversation with Jack "Chip" Bishop*, by Molly Lineberger, January 27, 2011, Center for Congregational Health, http://cntr4conghealth.wordpress.com/baptists-today-archives/interview-with-chip-bishop/.

[5]Steve Bagi, *pastorpain: my journey in burnout* (e-book, Palm Beach, Queensland, Australia: Actuate Consulting, 2008), 2, 10.

[6]Ibid., 102.

[7]See Chris Backert and Travis Collins, "Voices in the Local Church: Fresh Expressions of Church," *Evangelical Missions Quarterly*, 50, no. 3 (July, 2014). See also www.freshexpressionsus.org to get more information on fresh expressions.

Bibliography

Anderson, Lynn. *They Smell Like Sheep,* West Monroe, La.: Howard Publishing, 1997.

Anderson, Leith. *Leadership That Works*, Minneapolis: Bethany House, 1999.

Bagi, Steve. *pastorpain: my journey in burnout,* e-book, Palm Beach, Queensland, Australia: Actuate Consulting, 2008).

Barton, Ruth Haley. *Pursuing God's Will Together*, Downers Grove, Ill.: InterVarsity Press, 2012.

Bauer, Walter. *A Greek-English Lexicon of the New Testament*, Chicago: The University of Chicago Press, 1957.

Bishop, Chip. *Interview with Chip Bishop, On Changing from Senior Pastor to Financial Advisor: A Conversation with Jack "Chip" Bishop*, by Molly Lineberger, January 27, 2011, Center for Congregational Health, http://cntr4conghealth.wordpress.com/baptists-today-archives/interview-with-chip-bishop/.

Blackaby, Henry, and Richard Blackaby. *Spiritual Leadership*, Nashville: Broadman & Holman, 2001.

Blackaby, Tom. *Experiencing God's Love,* Birmingham: New Hope Publishers, 2011.

Blanchard, Ken, Bill Hybels, and Phil Hodges, *Leadership by the Book*. New York: William Morrow and Company, 1999.

Boers, Arthur Paul. *Never Call Them Jerks,* Washington, D.C.: Alban Institute, 1999.

Bonhoeffer, Dietrich. *Cost of Discipleship*, New York: Touchstone, 1995.

_____.*Life Together*, New York: Harper & Row, 1954.

Bratcher, Edward. *The Walk on Water Syndrome,* Waco: Word, 1984.

Bullard, George. *What If It Really Is the Pastor's Fault?* The Columbia Partnership, May 22, 2012.

Carver, W. O. *Acts of the Apostles*, Nashville: Broadman Press, 1916.

Chandler, Charles. "Forced Termination Leaves Deep Scars on Ministers' Spouses," Unpublished paper.

Cloud, Henry, John Townsend. *How To Have That Difficult Conversation You've Been Avoiding*, Grand Rapids, Mich.: Zondervan, 2003.

Colson, Jake. *So You Don't Want To Go To Church Anymore*, Los Angeles: Windblown Media, 2006.

Collins, Travis. *Directionally Challenged*, Birmingham: New Hope, 2006.

Covey, Stephen. *First Things First*, New York: Simon & Schuster, 1994.

_____.*The 7 Habits of Highly Effective People*, New York: Fireside, 1987.

Cordeiro, Wayne. *Leading on Empty*, Minneapolis: Bethany House, 2009.

Daniel, Lillian, and Martin B. Copenhavor. *This Odd & Wondrous Calling*. Grand Rapids, Mich.: William B. Eerdmans, 2009.

Drumheller, Kristina. "The Bullied Pulpit: The Church as a Site for Workplace Bullying," 2009 (http://connection.ebscohost.com/c/articles/54435208/bullied-pulpit-church-as-site-workplace-bullying).

Ferguson, Sheri S. "Clergy Compassion Fatigue," *Family Therapy Magazine* (March/April 2007).

Foster, Richard. *Celebration of Discipline*, New York: Harper Collins, 1978.

Girzone, Joseph. *Joshua* , New York: Macmillan, 1987.

Gledhill, Ruth. "Clergy and Ministers Need Protection from Church Bullying, Unite Union Says," BishopAccountability. org, 2004. (http://www.bishop-accountability.org/news2010/01_02/2010_01_04_Gledhill_ClergyAnd.htm).

Greenfield, Guy. *The Wounded Minister,* Grand Rapids, Mich.: Baker Books, 2001.

Gulley, Philip. *Just Shy of Harmony*, New York: HarperCollins, 2002.

Hull, Bill. *The Disciple-Making Pastor,* Grand Rapids, Mich.: Fleming H. Revell, 1988.

Hybels, Bill. *Honest to God*, Grand Rapids, Mich.: Zondervan, 1990.

Jackson, Anne. *Mad Church Disease*, Grand Rapids, Mich.: Zondervan, 2009.

Jones, Laurie Beth. *Jesus CEO*, New York: Hyperion, 1994.

Killinger, John. *Seven Things They Don't Tell You in Seminary*, New York: Crossroad, 2006.

King, Jr., Martin Luther. *The Papers of Martin Luther King, Jr., Volume VI*, Clayborne Carson, Senior Editor, Berkley: University of California Press, 2007.

Klaas, Alan C. and Cheryl D. Klaas. *Quiet Conversations*, Kansas City: Mission Growth Publishing, 2000.

Kriegbaum, Richard. *Leadership Prayers*, Carol Stream, Ill.: Tyndale House, 1998.

Ladd, George Eldon. *A Theology of the New Testament*, Grand Rapids, Mich.: William B. Eerdmans, 1974.

Leas, Speed. *Leading Your Church Through Conflict and Reconciliation*, Minneapolis: Bethany House, 1997.

MacDonald, Gordon. *The Life God Blesses*, Nashville: Thomas Nelson, 1994.

_____.*Who Stole My Church?*, Nashville: Thomas Nelson, 2007.

Macgregor, C.H.C. "Acts," *The Interpreter's Bible* (Nashville: Abingdon Press, 1954.

Maxwell, John. *Developing the Leader Within You*, Nashville: Thomas Nelson Publishers, 1993.

McKeever, Joe. "This Pastor Gives 100 Tips for Leaders That Everyone in Ministry Should Know," (http://www.churchleaders.com/pastors/pastor-articles/170770-joe-mckeever-pastor-gives-100-tips-for-leaders-that-everyone-in-ministry-should-know.html).

McIntosh, Jon. ChurchLeaders.com, "6 Reasons Why Pastors Want to Quit on Mondays"; (http://www.churchleaders.com/pastors/pastor-articles/150317-jon-mcintosh-six-reasons-why-pastors-want-to-quit-on-mondays.html).

McNeal, Reggie. *A Work of Heart*, San Francisco: Jossey-Bass, 2000.

Miller, Calvin. *Letters to a Young Pastor*. Colorado Springs: David C. Cook, 2011.

Ortberg, John. *If You Want to Walk on Water, You've Got to Get Out of the Boat*, Grand Rapids, Mich.: Zondervan, 2001.

Osei-Mensah, Gottfried. *Wanted: Servant Leaders*, Achimota, Ghana: African Christian Press, 1996.

Peck, Scott. *People of the Lie*, New York: Simon & Schuster, 1983.

Patterson, Ben. *Leading Your Church Through Conflict and Reconciliation*, Marshall Shelley, general editor, Minneapolis: Bethany House, 1997.

Patterson, Kerry, Joseph Grenny, Ron McMillan, and Al Switzler. *Crucial Confrontation: Tools for Resolving Broken Promises, Violated Expectations, and Bad Behavior*, New York: McGraw-Hill, 2005.

_____.*Crucial Conversations: Tools for Talking When the Stakes are High*, New York: McGraw-Hill, 2002;

Peterson, Eugene. *The Pastor*, New York: Harper One, 2011.

_____.*Under the Unpredictable Plant*, Grand Rapids, Mich.: William B. Eerdmans, 1992.

Phillips, Donald T. *Lincoln on Leadership*, New York: Warner Books, 1992.

Pinion, Gary L. *Crushed: The Perilous Side of Ministry.* Springfield, Mo.: 21st Century Press, 2008.

Robinson, Marilynne. *Gilead*, New York: Picador, 2004.

Ronsvalle, John, and Sylvia Ronsvalle. *Behind the Stained Glass Windows*, Grand Rapids, Mich.: Baker Books, 1996.

Sanders, J. Oswald. *Spiritual Leadership*, Chicago: Moody Press, 1967.

Scazzero, Peter. *The Emotionally Healthy Church*, Grand Rapids, Mich.: Zondervan, 2010.

Self, Bill. *Defining Moments*, Lima, Ohio: CSS Publishing, 1999.

_____.*Surviving the Stained Glass Jungle*, Macon: Mercer University Press, 2011.

Shelley, Marshall. *Leading Your Church Through Conflict and Reconciliation*, Marshall Shelley, general editor, Minneapolis: Bethany House, 1997.

Sherman, Daniel. *Pastor Burnout Workbook*, e-book, PastorBurnout.com, 2011.

Schuller, Robert. *Tough Times Never Last, But Tough People Do*, Nashville: Thomas Nelson, 1983.

Smith, Kathleen S. *Stilling the Storm: Worship and Congregational Leadership in Difficult Times*, Herndon, Va.: Alban, 2006.

Smith. T.C. "Acts," *The Broadman Bible Commentary*, Nashville: Broadman Press, 1970.

Sevig, Julie B., "Bullying the Pastor," The Lutheran, February, 2011 (http://www.thelutheran.org/article/article.cfm?article_id=9636&key=92852494).

Shankleman, Martin. "Clergy Bullying Rife," John Mark Ministries, 2010 (http://jmm.aaa.net.au/articles/23204.htm).

Smith, Kathleen. *Stilling the Storm: Worship and Congregational Leadership in Difficult Times*, Herndon, Va.: The Alban Institute, 2006.

Steinke, Peter L. *Congregational Leadership in Anxious Times*, Herndon, Va.: Alban, 2006.

Taylor, Barbara Brown. *Leaving Church*, San Francisco: Harper San Francisco, 2006.

Traylor, Ted. "Water from Home," Leadership Journal (Fall 2004) (http://www.christianitytoday.com/le/2004/fall/19.43.html)

Vitello, Paul. "Taking a Break from the Lord's Work," *The New York Times*, August 1, 2010.

Warner, Greg. *USA Today*, October 28, 2009.

Webb, William. *Slaves, Women and Homosexuals: Exploring the Hermeneutics of Cultural Analysis*, Downers Grove: Ill., InterVarsity Press, 2001.

Webber, Robert E. *Younger Evangelicals*, Grand Rapids, Mich.: Baker Books, 2002.

Wesley, Charles. *And Can It Be That I Should Gain?*, 1738.

Wiersbe, Warren. *Be Obedient*, Wheaton, Ill.: Victor Books, 1991.

_____.*The Bible Exposition Commentary*, Wheaton, Ill.: Victor Books, 1989.

Willimon, William. "Acts," *Interpretation* Commentary, Atlanta: John Knox Press, 1988.

_____.*Changing Lives Through Preaching and Worship*. Grand Rapids, Mich.: Zondervan, 1995.

_____.*The Collected Sermons of William H. Willimon*, Louisville: Westminster John Knox Press, 2011.

Wilson, Michael Todd, and Brad Hoffman. *Preventing Ministry Failure*, Downer's Grove, Ill.: InterVarsity Press, 2007.

Witt, Lance. Replenish. Grand Rapids, Mich.: Baker Books, 2011.

http://www.csmonitor.com/Photo-Galleries/In-Pictures/The-10-happiest-jobs (2011)

The Wholehearted Church Planter

Leadership from the Inside Out

by Allan Karr and Linda Bergquist

The most essential criteria for church planters are not skill-based, nor personality driven, but character-centric and rooted in the Great Commandment. The authors of *The Wholehearted Church Planter* insist that church-planting proficiencies flow best from those who truly know and love God, people, and in an appropriate way, themselves. If the authors are correct, the potential for multiplying leaders and reproducing new churches is greatly enhanced. It means that ordinary Christians can evangelize, disciple, and gather people into all kinds of new communities of faith. They can impact church-planting movements in ways they never imagined. This book does not disregard the importance of training or the role of the professional, but it calls for a broader, deeper discernment of whom is being called by God to start new congregations.

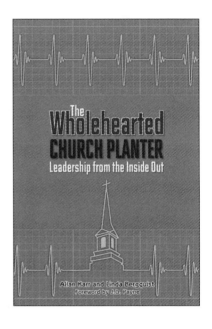

Print 9780827243026
EPUB 9780827243033
EPDF 9780827243040

So Much Better

How Thousands of Pastors Help Each Other Thrive

by The Sustaining Pastoral Excellence Peer Learning Project
Penny Long Marler • D. Bruce Roberts • Janet Maykus
James Bowers • Larry Dill • Brenda K. Harewood
Richard Hester • Sheila Kirton-Robbins • Marianne LaBarre
Lis Van Harten • Kelli Walker-Jones

Meant to both inspire and inform pastoral leaders, *So Much Better* examines the impact of peer group participation on pastoral leaders, their families, and ministries.

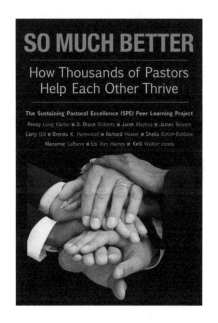

This book goes beyond numbers and data by breathing life into the statistical bones. At this book's heart are seven peer group models including stories and examples from participants, families, and church members. Also featured is information about peer group recruitment, leadership, content, and structure, and practical advice about the cost, sustainability, and evaluation of peer groups.

So Much Better can change the way you think about and perform your ministry and lead you to a life that is—well, so much better.

Print 9780827235243
EPUB 9780827235250
EPDF 9780827235267

TCP www.TCPBooks.com

Save 20% and support the authors and non-profit, faith-based publishing when you order online at www.TCPBooks.com

Leading Congregations through Crisis

by Gregory L. Hunt

On July 12, 2009, 23 youth and adult sponsors from First Baptist Church in Shreveport, La., were involved in a tragic bus accident, leaving two dead and others seriously injured. Rev. Gregory Hunt suddenly found himself leading a congregation in crisis.

From that grueling experience, Hunt has crafted a book pastors need to read even as they hope they'll never have to use it.

Ten different types of crises, ranging from violence to natural disasters to internal congregational strife, provide insight on how to lead congregations through harrowing times into healthy futures.

Print 9780827221703
EPUB 9780827221710
EPDF 9780827221727

Named as a 2012 Top Ten Book for Parish Ministry by the Academy of Parish Clergy

LEADING CONGREGATIONS
THROUGH CRISIS

GREGORY L. HUNT

The Calling of Congregational Leadership

Being, Knowing, Doing Ministry

by Larry L. McSwain

Leading is a calling from God, but that doesn't mean it is easy. There are choices to be made about what your congregation believes, how your church organizes for effective ministry, and how your church serves the settings of which you are a part. The good news is that others have gone before you.

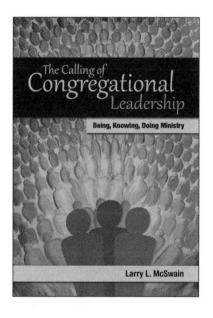

Rooted in research, *The Calling of Congregational Leadership* teaches a three-pronged approach to congregational leadership: being a good leader, the knowledge needed by the leader, and the managing of ministry leadership. By using this practical, holistic approach to leading congregations, McSwain shows you how to use your church's potential for conveying the power of God in the lives you touch.

Print 9780827205314
EPUB 9780827205321
EPDF 9780827205338

www.TCPBooks.com

Save 20% and support the authors and non-profit, faith-based publishing when you order online at www.TCPBooks.com

Recovering Hope for Your Church

Moving beyond Maintenance and Missional to Incarnational Engagement

by Edward H. Hammett

"Why?" seems to be on the lips of many church, judicatory, and denominational leaders today.

"Why has our church plateaued?"

"Why are so few young leaders going into church-based ministries?"

"Why are so few interested in church these days?"

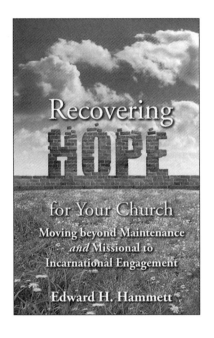

Recovering Hope for Your Church uncovers the "whys," creating space to embrace new realities, commit to the tough road of recovery, and develop new skills, structures, and ministry designs through a process of spiritual discernment, congregational coaching, and a deeper reliance on the work and ministry of the Holy Spirit.

Eddie Hammett, a Professional Certified Coach and Church and Clergy Coach for the Cooperative Baptist Fellowship of North Carolina, provides a step-by-step process of hope and health to encourage, guide, and inspire pastors, leaders, churches, regions, and denominations that recovery of hope is possible.

Print 9780827232280
EPUB 9780827232297
EPDF 9780827232303